Be Brave, Do Hard Things, Believe.

One Flag Football Team's Journey to #makingherstory

PC: Alfred Cornejo/Van Zantes Photography

The Aptos High School 2023 Inaugural Girls Flag Football Team

While every precaution has been taken in the preparation of this book, the publisher assumes no responsibility for errors or omissions, or for damages resulting from the use of the information contained herein.

BE BRAVE. DO HARD THINGS. BELIEVE.

First edition. September 7, 2024.

ISBN: 979-8227311610

Written by Denise Calafato Russo.

Table of Contents

To all the strong, powerful, athletic women who have fought
for gender equity in sports everywhere.

First Quarter: Prologue

Kick Off

On a hot and sunny Saturday afternoon in California, the scoreboard illuminated 7-0 in the Santa Cruz Coast Athletic League's (SCCAL) inaugural Girls Flag Football (GFF) championship game. With time running out, the Aptos High School (AHS) Mariner's defense needed to stop the opponent from scoring on this final drive to become the first SCCAL champions, undefeated in the league. The secondary patiently waited to cover any deep balls thrown their way. The middle backs were highly alert for trick plays like flea flickers and reverse handoffs. The rusher was on their toes, waiting for their signal from the sideline. Rush, delay, blitz? Everyone in the stadium felt the desire to win. Not because there was regional or state championships on the line, college scholarships that might depend on it, or any other tangible reason to need to finish with the W. As a new sport, those opportunities had not <yet> emerged. This team wanted to win for each other, the community they had created, the hard work they had completed, and as a part of #makingherstory. And so, with a pressure that was palpable, everyone waited as the opponent's team broke the huddle, snapped the ball, and.......

But this story isn't about the result of this game or the season. It's about the camaraderie of football. It is about giving up Saturday mornings and family dinner time to practice with your team. It is about the challenge of learning to run routes, take handoffs, and intercept an oddly shaped ball. It is about learning new rules and an entire playbook. It is about learning the language and nuances of a sport historically unfamiliar to high school girls. It is about a diverse group of players who bravely went from tentative strangers to cohesive teammates to good friends, who built each other up and supported each other's achievements. And it is about making inroads and being heard on the path to gender equity (#makingherstory), as experienced by players and coaches.

Our story is one of "empowHerment." It addresses the ongoing movement for gender parity through the lens of sport. It progresses forward from the female athletes and the allies who have supported women in athletics. It emerges from the shadows of athletes like Kathrine Switzer, the first woman to run the Boston Marathon as an official runner, and Billie Jean King and her advocacy that led to the U.S. Open becoming the first major tennis tournament to offer equal monetary rewards to both genders. It continues from the USWNT's (United States Women's National Soccer Team) fight for "Equal pay! Equal pay!" And it is based in Title IX, U.S. legislation passed in 1972 to prevent discrimination based on sex in education programs, including increasing participation of girls in youth, high school, and college sports.

Despite these advancements, disparities continue to exist. According to an article by the Gatorade Sports Science Institute, the participation of girls and women in sports remains inequitable. The cause of this inequity is multifactorial. This article describes the uneven distribution of resources, funding, and promotion of girl's and women's sports across all groups. Marginalized communities continue to have fewer opportunities to participate in sports. The media also continues to emphasize men's sports with content and coverage, despite the 2023 Women's NCAA Basketball Championship game viewership crushing the men's competition and with 65% of the USA's gold medals at the 2024 Summer Olympics being won by women. Sports science is also behind for women, with Christine Yu discussing the lack of scientific research on female athletes in her book "Up to Speed: The Groundbreaking Science of Women Athletes." Please note that we recognize inequity extends beyond the traditional male/female classifications, but the focus of our story is on girls and women. Female athletes must continue to use their voices and athleticism to reduce the gender equity gap in sports.

In the era of Caitlin Clark, Serena Williams, Simone Biles, Alex Morgan, and so many others, gender equity is the background of our story. In these pages, athletes share their experiences of being brave, doing hard things, and believing in their journey of empowHerment. For many of our athletes, this season was their first opportunity to play competitively with the "pigskin on the gridiron." Some had their interest sparked in 2020 at the local junior highs with a few short weeks of practice before COVID-19 took sports and social systems away from them. Others had thrown footballs with their family or watched their brothers play without a feasible outlet for being a competitive team member. Regardless of their experience, these athletes bravely came to a sport they described as being a space primarily for boys, learning an unfamiliar language (a route tree, pick-6, a PAT, and why is a safety both a player and a play that earns points) while playing this new-to-them game. Led by a staff of women coaches, these athletes did the hard work of building a team and a program in the inaugural year, setting the stage for women supporting women on the ongoing road to gender equity through the sport of flag football.

But why has flag football become one of the world's fastest-growing sports? Flag football is not a new sport. It is a variant of American football that started on United States military bases during WWII. Soldiers played a form of touch football to maintain physical fitness while avoiding injury. After the war, these military members brought the game back home to the US which led to the initial flag football league. Flag football has grown tremendously since then, with various leagues emerging to support both men and women in the sport. Leagues include the National Touch Football League (1960s), The United States Flag Football Association (1981), the United States Flag and Touch Football League (1991), and the National Intramural and

Recreational Sports Association flag football league. Recreational flag football leagues also exist for children, including a league sponsored by the National Football League (NFL) that has programs in every state. According to one report, there has been a 63% increase in the number of girls ages 6-17 playing flag football since 2019, with women now comprising 25% of the athletes in the sport.

Flag football is also played on the international stage. The International Federation of American Football (IFAF) is responsible for the global growth of tackle and flag football. The International Women's Flag Football Association (IWFFA), founded in 1997, is an organization led by women for women, offering flag football tournaments worldwide. The first world championship games for men's and women's teams were held in 2002. Twenty years later, flag football was added to the 2022 World Games. In 2023, the IFAF and the NFL lobbied for flag football to be added to the Olympics, and in late 2023, the International Olympic Committee (IOC) approved it for the 2028 games. This support has been one of the keys to propelling GFF forward.

In the same year that flag football was approved as a future Olympic sport, the CIF sanctioned flag football for girls in high school. Adding this sport provides girls with a safer and less costly version of football that is accessible and inclusive, contributing to its popularity. This sanctioning of GFF in California occurred almost 20 years after Florida sanctioned it as a high school sport. As of the writing of this book, 12 states have sanctioned GFF (Florida, Alabama, Georgia, Nevada, Alaska, New York, Arizona, Illinois, California, Colorado, Montana, and Hawaii), with 17 other states in various stages of pilot programs at their high schools. Girls Flag Football is also breaking barriers as an emerging collegiate sport option in the USA, sanctioned as a varsity sport in over 15 NAIA colleges in 2024, with the Atlantic East Conference (DIII) expected to be the first NCAA conference to offer women's flag football in 2025. Colleges with women's flag football are in Georgia, Florida, Missouri, Kansas, Tennessee, Wisconsin, Nebraska, Louisiana, Minnesota, Mississippi, and California (La Sierra University), with some athletic aid available to interested athletes. Collectively, these opportunities to play flag football have contributed to the skyrocketing interest in girls flag football, with ~500,000 girls playing flag football in 2023, a 63% increase since 2019.

Locally, the players interviewed in this book had limited flag football experience. In their biographies, you will see that many had not previously played football. For those who had experience, it was with our school district, which was progressive in offering flag football as a junior high sport. Just one player, Emi, had participated in the local NFL Central Coast Flag Football League. Our team was diverse in other ways as well, representing different grade levels, ethnicities, sexual orientations, socio-economic statuses, and athletic experiences. These girls came together to play flag football for various reasons. Some came with a long love of football, excited to participate in a non-contact version. Others were interested in having a new athletic experience. A couple of athletes were quiet and introverted and hoping to make friends. Quite a few were looking to find relief from the anxiety and depression that followed us from the pandemic shutdowns.

Together we faced various challenges that may have resulted from being girls in a new sport. We had to speak assertively to claim practice space on the field historically reserved for boys in the season of Friday Night Lights. We had to learn to speak firmly but respectfully to referees when rules were in question. "Respectfully, ref, that was a spin which is against the rules," stated team Captain Izzy, who knew all the rules. We had to learn to SPEAK UP and BE SEEN when we felt small and unheard when discussing equitable schedules, field dimensions, or the rules. Over our months together, these challenges and our conversations about them helped us develop into friends, a community, and a team. Each person came with their own history, voids, and agenda for being a part of this team.

In these interviews, the coaches and players tell their stories of breaking down barriers with an opportunity to play a version of a sport typically played by boys and men. Some, like Siena, mentioned an earlier interest in football that they couldn't pursue due to the safety concerns of being tackled by people who generally outsized them. Others, like Maddie B and Nancy, noted that even if they played tackle football, they had observed they were unlikely to receive playing time in this male-dominated sport. Together, this team developed skills on and off the field that led them to believe in themselves and their teammates on their journey of gender equity. Players described the support they felt from their team and as a group of girls coached by a group of women. Many reflected on flag football's inroads towards creating gender equity in sports for women. Through an analysis of each of their interviews, I share what we collectively noted on the path to bravely doing the hard thing of believing in #makingherstory.

This book includes the stories and voices of this team. Coaches and players chose to participate by completing a written or in-person interview. *I then edited each interview, maintaining the voice of each player, and presented these at the start of each chapter, italicizing any voice that wasn't my own.* I then include my reflection on each of these team members. The chapter concludes with a perception of the words "Be brave, do hard things, believe," as described or demonstrated by each person. As you read through the pages, you will have an opportunity to "play along" to see if you can guess which player was given which "the one who…" title and even ask yourself what title you might have received if you had been part of the team.

Oh, and how did the championship game end? Keep reading……

Roster

Coaches

Head Coach, Denise Russo

Coach, Angela Chmelicek

Coach, Gabriella Russo

Coach, Gabby Fely

Players

Alexa

Angelique

Annika

Ashlyn

Ava (Gavin)

Dakota

Elenah

Ellie

Emi

Gaby

Izzy

Janelle

Julia

June

Lauren

Maddie

Madi

Mia

Mikayla

Nancy

Natasha

Nina

Siena

Valerie

Gratitude by Head Coach Denise Russo

This journey would not have been possible without quite a few people, some I know and others I do not, but I thank you just the same. My apologies to any I didn't specifically list in these thank yous.

First, I need to recognize the California Interscholastic Federation (CIF). As the state's governing body for high school sports, its mission (as stated on its website) is that "every student in California has a unique opportunity to participate and experience being a part of a school team or student organization." That includes over 50 years of supporting Title IX. They voted unanimously in early 2023 to add Girls' Flag Football (GFF) as a statewide sanctioned sport.

Next, I thank the Santa Cruz County Athletics League (SCCAL), which agreed to include GFF in its first year of sanctioning. Other leagues delayed their start, but under the leadership of Mark Dorfman, the SCCAL was progressive and agreed to have teams in 2023, even when there were questions about scheduling, referee availability, coaches, and field space.

At Aptos High School (AHS), thank you, Principal Dr. Alison Hanks Sloan, for supporting the inclusion of GFF in 2023. She and many of the faculty and staff, including the activities director (Ryane Ortiz), the theater manager (Luke Hess), the yearbook director (Stacy Aronovici), and the tackle football program, were supportive of these students and this team. There are far too many names to list all the faculty and staff supporters at AHS, but the team is grateful to all of you!

Our exceptional athletic director, Travis Fox, lobbied to ensure we had a team and a league in this inaugural year. He spent many hours over multiple lunches guiding this novice varsity coach, giving QB tips to players, and being the voice of AHS GFF when announcing our home games. When I had to "Be Brave and Do Hard Things," he was the one who "Believed."

We wouldn't be the team that we are without Scott Russo. He has been my role model of how to treat athletes, implementing the philosophy that you don't learn if you aren't in the games. While playing time isn't equal at the varsity level, treating all players respectfully remains imperative. As a defensive coordinator in my previous flag football coaching experiences, I had never called a play, let alone drawn one up. Collectively, my coaching assistants had two seasons of coaching GFF. There was a lot to learn, and Scott took on the role of coach consultant, teaching us so that we could teach the players.

Thank you to the families, friends, and community who supported this team. We had a budget of $0 to pay for uniforms and equipment. Hotsource Yoga made a sizable donation to pay for the uniforms. Family members, including my own mom and stepdad, and friends provided donations. Others participated in various fundraiser activities that allowed us to purchase footballs, flags, cones, play wristbands, etc. In addition, they were vocal at our games and provided positive input along the way.

A special thanks to Carla Sikand, a past student of mine who took an interest in this project when we met one day to discuss her career opportunities. And to my sister Suzanne Russo, who, despite the many challenges she faced while I was writing, always took time to answer my questions or make a phone call. Both women helped me organize and expand on my words in a way that makes sense to the reader.

Lastly, I have to thank this team. Coaches Angela, Gabriella, and Gabby were volunteers this year, as there was no budget for the coaching staff. They gave up countless hours to be here for these players, and their only compensation was the joy of the experience and a few free dinners. Thank you to our players for all the sacrifices I know you made. Some of you had to step away from another sport to be a part of GFF. Many of you had to cram homework in between school and our late evening practices. It was a challenge to balance academics when you got home well after sunset, still needing to eat dinner before finishing homework. These were long days for all of us. The journey was worth it.

Denise Russo, Head Coach

Play Along

At our awards night, we gave each player a "The one who...." title. For fun, we encourage you to use this checklist as you read our story to decide which player earned which title.

o The one most likely not to get called for flag-guarding

o The one most likely to be a future coach

o The one most likely to catch every QB's pass

o The one most likely to forget her water bottle

o The one most likely to lower her shoulder

o The one most likely to make Coach Denise do a jig

o The one most likely to play flag football in Europe

o The one most likely to tackle the QB

o The one most likely to throw the long ball

o The one most likely to give her teammates or coach a hug

o The one who always brings positivity to the field

o The one who embodies a goldfish

o The one who embodies being a football player

o The one who found her spot at safety

o The one who gets along with everyone

o The one who gets knocked over and pops right back up

o The one who lights up the team with happy

o The one who perseveres

o The one who quietly creates offensive success

- o The one who reminds us that football is fun

- o The one whose actions speak louder than words

- o The one whose face never lies

- o The one whose hips DO lie

- o The one you can depend on

Second Quarter: The Coaches

Coach Denise Russo

- Position: Head Coach, Defensive Coordinator
- Previous Seasons Coached Flag Football: 15+
- Seasons Played Flag Football: 0
- Other Sports Coached: Soccer, Cross Country, Track and Field
- Three Words That Describe Denise: Empathetic, Equity-Minded, Energetic

As a high school athlete, I was an equestrian. My "team" consisted of husband-and-wife trainers and other junior riders in the barn. We earned our awards individually, but ribbons hanging outside the tack room were good advertisements for our program. Although we competed against each other in classes, we functioned as a "family" of people who supported one another. With my barn family, I went through various hardships, including crushing disappointment when my horse went lame at Nationals, navigating the aftermath of divorced parents, friend group drama, and the insecurity of not believing I was good enough (imposter syndrome, I would learn later as the term for this). With this family, I felt safe and brave. With them I learned the importance of a supportive team for navigating life's challenges.

It was in this space that I first observed gender inequity in sports. A quick Google search shows that women are more likely to be involved in equestrian activities than men. One article mentioned it as "gender-lopsided" towards women. However, most successful trainers in the Arabian horse business were men. In the blue-ribbon circle, implicit gender inequity appeared to exist. In some sports, there is a clear winner: the first runner across the finish line, the team with the most points on the scoreboard, or the person who jumped the furthest. Other sports are subjective in scoring, as with pleasure horse showing. I was lucky to have found a well-trained, exceptionally well-moving horse with a winning record. But there were classes where, despite having a well-executed ride, we came in second, behind a male rider. Multiple comments from strangers after class were "You were robbed," or "I definitely thought you and your horse should have won." I don't think I recognized inequity at this age, but looking back, I see it existed.

On my non-traditional college path, I veered away from any science, technology, engineering, or mathematics (STEM) major. I didn't have the confidence that women did well in these topics. My boyfriend reinforced this by recommending I take a different route when I contemplated changing to a science-based major. He told me that the chemistry would be too difficult for me. I worked hard, proved him wrong, and earned the highest chemistry exam grade. I continued with the major but not the boyfriend. After college, I was excited to join the ICU medical team as a clinical dietitian. I would get to work early to review charts in preparation for participating in rounds and making recommendations for medical nutrition therapy in the same way that the male respiratory therapist would make recommendations. One day, our attending physician asked me, "When did the dietitian become so assertive?" I replied, "We call it being proactive." This moment solidified for me the gender inequity of language we use to describe the actions of women.

As a college professor, I took these lessons into my classroom. My teaching methods started traditional (lecture, memorize, test, repeat) as I again navigated imposter syndrome, this time as an instructor. Working at various Hispanic-serving Institutions in California, I became aware of the education disparity that existed through race/ethnicity, socioeconomic status, sexual orientation, body shape, sex, and gender. As I grew in my career, I learned about student-focused teaching practices to support historically underrepresented students in STEM majors, including people of color and women. I investigated methods focused on learning rather than teaching and even earned a doctorate studying these principles. Bias and disparity are sometimes subtle, but if you really open your eyes and heart, you can see it. What I learned in my research was the significance of creating a supportive community (professor<->student<->student) to create student success. Finding courage in the knowledge that I had acquired, I stepped out of the traditional teaching box. I transitioned my classes to student-focused learning techniques to support the education success of historically underrepresented populations in STEM.

When I started coaching a team sport, I revisited imposter syndrome. I had only had one season of youth soccer playing experience when I was asked to be a coach. I braved my insecurities and began to coach and learn alongside Coach David. This path eventually led to my coaching flag football at the local junior high. If you just thought, "Oh, I bet that really made her feel that imposter insecurity," you were right! Growing up a fan of football (Go Niners!), this was the sport I was most excited to coach despite having no experience playing football. This time, my support was my husband, who had been coaching flag football for years. I learned flag football skills as I coached alongside him for over a decade. I implemented my learner-focused teaching methods to build our team. When my husband retired from coaching flag football, I continued, always saying, "I am a good junior high coach, but I wouldn't want to be a varsity high school coach."

Then, the California Interscholastic Federation (CIF) added Girls Flag Football (GFF) as a varsity high school sport. With my experience at the junior high, I was the likely candidate to be the head coach of our high school team. This position felt like my teaching world was aligning with my coaching world. I had the opportunity to create a supportive team environment while addressing an area of gender inequity in sports. I was excited to be "#makingherstory." But in my head were all those insecurities that come with "Am I good enough?" and "Do I really know what I am doing?" I lost more than one night's sleep on this journey and had to battle the knowledge I'd coach against others who knew more about football. Bravely, I accepted the challenge and, in the footsteps of so many strong women, did the hard thing of continuing to push the gender equity gap while leading a TEAM of women who supported one another on a field historically dominated by men.

When we first came together for summer conditioning practices, I focused on learning football and building our team. But, if there were a song that played as the backdrop of this story, it would be "The Man" by Taylor Swift. The first hint that I would need to be "a fearless leader" was when scheduling field space for our practices in the fall. Our school has two fields. One is the turf (Trevin Dilfer) football field under the lights where we would play our games. The other is the smaller gopher-hole-ridden grass (Bobby Salazar) field, which lacks lights and needs maintenance. When the realization set in that the varsity GFF team would need field space at the same time as tackle teams, some, including my husband, said, "Your team can practice on the Salazar field. You don't need the turf." There it was. The message that the Girls Flag Football team was less important than the male-dominated tackle team was loud and clear.

My players, a few with boyfriends on that tackle team, asked me, "Coach Denise, why do we have to practice on the grass while the boys' teams are on the turf?" I firmly replied, "We do not. We are a varsity team and have equal priority to the turf." Working with our athletic director, I initially navigated this passively, being mindful of the existing practice schedule of the tackle football teams and asking for space so as not to disrupt their schedule. Tackle football had historically had the full field at least one night/week to practice kick-off returns, and I tried to accommodate that. As the parent of a graduated football player, I understood the importance of practice space for special teams. But I was receiving inconsistent messages about the schedule that was making me change my schedule. Finally, instead of asking when it worked for me to have my practice, I got brave and told our athletic director WHEN I was holding my practices and finalized my schedule.

As I continue with this section, it's important to note that I don't think the conflicts I experienced were overtly due to us being a girls team coached by women. Having to accommodate a new team with the field space available was a challenge at any school. But gender inequity is often implicit, and the most well-meaning of humans contribute to it. Someone described my firm request for field space as being "assertive" (there it is again), but other teams encroached into our space when I didn't set boundaries around our practice times.

On our first day of practice, we excitedly waited in a corner of the end zone for our start time. My players were getting hydrated, talking, and laughing as they transitioned from student to athlete. As our start time approached, it didn't appear that the tackle team would be vacating the field in time for us to start. My players looked at me expectantly. What were we going to do? Wait, and start late? Take off our cleats and squeeze in together to warm up on the track? I knew this was a defining moment for our season and for me as a role model for equity. So, I stood tall (not an easy act at just under 5' 2"), walked up to the tackle coach, and firmly said to him, "We are starting our practice, so please (I think I said please, I hope I said please) move out of our practice space." He moved and later apologized. It wasn't the only time I ever had a field conflict. Sometimes, I felt I let my team down when I didn't hold firm to commanding our scheduled space. But I always followed that up with a conversation with the other coach so that when we returned to the field it was in our scheduled space. My hope is that I role modeled respectful interaction that led to just outcomes.

The practice field wasn't the only place I had to work to have the voices of my female coaching staff heard. I need to preface that I believe being a referee is a thankless and challenging job. I don't know how they see everything. I know that I undoubtedly cannot. Their difficulties were further complicated by GFF being a new sport with multiple versions of the rules shared as the season developed. There were plenty of opportunities for rule confusion. In fact, before each game, the coaches and refs met to discuss the rules such as "Which version of the spin rule are we using?" I have found this section of the book the most challenging to write. The men we work with mean no harm and are often out there as strong supporters of our girls in sports. As our allies, they are working with us to advance female participation in athletics. I have years of sideline experience observing referees stand by their decisions, no matter the gender of the coach questioning the call. But bias is often implicit and buried deep in a culture of sports masculinity. I believe that while the situations I describe are not intentional, they were influenced by gender bias. They arise from a history of male dominance in sports, which continually creates a background for women to have to speak loudly ("Equal pay! Equal pay!") to be heard and seen.

As a female head coach, I have often felt the referees didn't hear me. I recognize this is subjective. But, coaching with my husband for years, it wasn't unusual for me to question a call, be ignored, and then have my husband repeat the same question, and the ref would respond. In one junior high game, the opposing team's coach challenged the referee about an end zone call that did not go his way. He summoned the referee over to watch a playback on a video a parent had taken. I called out to the ref, "Hey, ref, there is no instant replay in junior high!" The referee ignored my multiple escalating reminders that instant replay isn't allowed as he continued to the sideline to view the video. Despite speaking very loudly and walking onto the field after him, I was ignored. I had to ask someone to get Mike, my athletic director, to come to the field to advocate for my team. Once Mike talked to the referee, he relented, and whatever was on the video footage was never discussed. But my players noticed that the referee had ignored me and listened to Mike.

In a different game, a referee approached me during halftime to explain his unique method of marking the rush on the field. I requested to defer this conversation as I needed to make coaching adjustments with my team since we only had a short half-time. He demanded that I listen to what he had to say and wouldn't leave my side. During this half-time break, he only gave this explanation on my sideline with two female coaches and never spoke to the other team's male coaching staff. It was difficult to understand why we would get different treatment.

When the AHS GFF varsity team stepped on the field in the inaugural game by a team in our league, we were nervous and excited. This night felt big on our road of #makingherstory. In the first few minutes of the game, Izzy ran the ball into the endzone for the first touchdown in this momentous game. Later, Sofia scored on a pick-6, and we earned two more points with a safety. With less than two minutes left in the game, we were ahead 14-12. We called a play to get the first down to position ourselves to run the time off the clock for a win. QB Gaby had already taken the option to run in this series, so, by rule, she could not run again. However, the quarterback is the person who takes the snap. We moved Gaby to a running back position where she could run or pass by taking the handoff from the person in the QB position. Seeing an open hole, she ran the ball and secured the first down. Securing the first down put us in a position to win by running the time off the clock. Our sideline erupted in cheers! As the head coach, I should have seen everything that happened in that play. But I missed the play as I turned my attention to subbing in players for the final 90 seconds of the game.

I didn't see that the ref had dropped the yellow flag. He penalized us for the quarterback running twice in a series. Team Captain Izzy quickly challenged that the runner, Gaby, hadn't been the quarterback on that play. Gaby had taken the handoff, not the snap. When the referee ignored the team captain, my offensive coordinator went onto the field to discuss what had happened. The referee didn't seem to be listening to what she said and dismissed our request for him to re-evaluate the penalty. The opponent moved to offense and ran a play. After that one play, the referee apologized, saying he had made the wrong call but couldn't change it now because he'd let a play run—the incorrect call and not being listened to rattled our team. We couldn't find our edge on defense. With just moments left in the game, we let the opponents into the end zone and lost the first game in our team's history. Keep this game in mind. You will read about it again through the eyes of several players in other chapters.

Just a few days later, we had our first league game. Before it started, both head coaches discussed the field set-up with the referees, identifying the first down marks and no run zones. When the referee miscalled a yardage gain, we called him over to review the field dimensions again. We discussed it a few times, and I showed him a drawing of the field with the league-approved dimensions, but he still could not understand. My husband was in attendance to give us support. Seeing confusion, he walked over with an identically marked drawing of the field and reviewed the dimensions with the referee. It was when my husband explained and showed the exact field dimensions that the referee finally understood.

By the middle of the season, a referee jokingly told me, "You are the one known for knowing the rules." Let me tell you about one of those rules.

The rule about the no-run zone is that no handoffs are allowed. "When the ball is snapped within the No Run Zone, it shall not be advanced beyond the LOS without first being passed forward or backward." In one of our final games of the season, where we had a comfortable lead, the opposing team handed off in the No Run Zone. The player that took the handoff then passed the ball. The illegal handoff confused my defense since they knew it was a penalty, and that confusion resulted in a touchdown for the other team. "Hey, ref," I said, "they aren't allowed to handoff in the No Run one." The ref countered that they had passed after the handoff. I said that wasn't the rule, but he ignored me and allowed the touchdown to stand. When the game ended, the opposing coach asked why I cared about that missed call since we were poised to win anyway at the point of the touchdown. It felt dismissive, and I wondered if such a mistake would be allowed if the game was male-dominated tackle and not girls flag football.

Various men also questioned my play-calling and coaching techniques during the season. I believe this is usually meant to be helpful and happens universally in sports, no matter the coach or team. Even Super Bowl coaches receive criticism of their play calling. I am not only grateful for help but actively seek it. In our home, with a daughter on the coaching staff and my husband, the coaches' trainer, we speak a lot about how I can better coach our team. But direct comments to my players like, "Hasn't your coach taught you how to rush?" and "Why are you holding the football like that? You need to do it this way," and "Why isn't she using the option?" are disparaging to my coaching staff. When this happens, I hear the Taylor Swift lyric, "I'm so sick of running as fast as I can, wondering if I'd get there quicker if I was a man?" I work to role model to my team how to take these comments, evaluate them, use what helps, and dismiss the rest.

These moments of feeling small and as if we have no voice are not unusual for women in sports. They are just examples of how our players and coaches experienced them. It is important to note that many people I have interacted with, including coaches, referees, and my husband, are allies in promoting gender equity in sports. The coaches of our tackle teams have come to games, complimented my players, and opened communication to navigate our shared space equitably. My husband now acknowledges our need to be on the turf. The referees take the time to review the rules before our game starts. One even saw my husband in the community and apologized for his interaction with me. Numerous men (coaches, referees, ADs, and community members) have verbally supported this sport for engaging girls in football. Taylor Swift may have facilitated an increase in women watching football, but I thank the CIF (and those in other states), the NFL, the IWFFA, the IOC, and our allies for their work toward gender equity.

Players' Audible

Coach Denise is a role model of what it means to be a powerful woman in today's society. She cares about her players and teaches me that no one else can decide my boundaries except me. She wants to build genuine relationships, creating a sense of "family" on the field. Coach Denise made us a team. (Mia P)

Coach Denise is full of positive energy and always looks on the bright side. I remember this specifically with our first loss. Instead of us "losing," she reminded us that this was just a way to see how we could improve. Coach Denise is a special coach who truly cares for each player and loves us like family. (Ellie)

As a multi-sport athlete, I've had many coaches in my lifetime; some are amazing, and others are not. But Coach Denise was one of the best I've ever had. When you first meet her, you may be intimidated by her strong voice, but she makes sure everyone has fun and gets playing time while building a supportive team. (Mikayla)

Be brave. Do hard things. Believe.

Each coach and player were asked how these words aligned with their experience on this team, included at the end of each chapter. These are the words I shared with my players when we competed in our last contest. I have given talks nationwide, completed a doctorate, and led workshops filled with higher education professionals. However, coaching a varsity sport was one of the most significant imposter challenges I have experienced. There were many days I didn't think I was good enough. Our first game confirmed my inadequacy. That game cost me a few nights of sleep as I anguished over my coaching failure and contemplated quitting. But it was also the turning point of my becoming a varsity head coach. I surrounded myself with supportive people and focused on the lessons we would take from that game. Learning flag football was imperative. Even more so, role-modeling for emerging adults on how to collaborate cohesively to support gender equity was the bigger purpose of playing flag football together. The players and coaches may not have known it when they first came to the field, but we were brave, we did hard things, and as we grew together, we accomplished all that we did because we believed.

Coach Angela Chmelicek

- Position: Offensive Coordinator

- Seasons Coached Flag Football: 1
- Seasons Played Flag Football: 1
- Position Played: Receiver, Safety
- Other Sports Coached: Track and Field
- Other Sports Played: Track and Field, Basketball

- Three Words That Describe Angela: Organized, Inspirational, Reliable

I grew up watching my grandfather referee football at the high school for as long as I can remember. It was always my favorite sport to watch, even though I didn't grow up playing on any sports teams. In 6th grade, I tried out for our track team, where I learned I had a strong throwing arm. I was excited to play my first team sport when I went out for flag football at the junior high. I enjoyed it so much that I joined the only all-girls team in our local Central Coast Flag Football league, and I played for both teams for the two years that was an option. I wanted to take advantage of playing for as long as possible since our high school didn't offer flag football or powder puff, and I knew that if I went out for tackle football, as a girl, I wouldn't get much playing time.

When Denise asked me to join the coaching staff at my alma mater, I was excited to have the opportunity to continue with my favorite sport. Although I didn't feel like I would fit in as a girl on the tackle football team in high school, I was the tackle football team manager. I looked forward to experiencing flag football again because I knew the time these players would have for this sport wouldn't last forever. I didn't anticipate the fulfillment of witnessing the players' growth as athletes and, more importantly, as a team. Friendships and camaraderie blossomed just as they had for me when I played in junior high. My longest friendships were with people I met on my flag football team. We grew close with laughter, hugs, and cheering on the sideline. In our last game, we could feel the energy from the team and the crowd, and when it ended, there was laughter and crying over what we had accomplished together. It warmed my heart to see how these players, who were recently strangers, now celebrated and supported each other as friends.

Despite my excitement, I was pretty terrified to be a varsity coach. I was inexperienced, and there was added pressure from all we needed to learn as we built a new program. Additionally, we were a coaching staff of all women, and although we had a lot of support, we faced sexism throughout the season. Being involved felt like we were making history (#makingherstory). Flag football provided another chance for girls to play sports. As we led our GFF team, we made a tiny change towards equity for our kids and community.

Players' Audible

Coach Angela has taught me that I should be authentically me. Like me, she is hard on herself, but she has taught me how important it is to care for myself. She has made me feel more confident on this team of girls who support each other. (Mia P)

Coach Angela is a supportive coach. She not only cheered me on in flag football but also texted me anytime I PR'd in throws and checked in with me if she heard I was injured. I am lucky to have a coach who supports me outside of just GFF. (Ellie)

Coach Denise

Angela is one of my "non-bio" children. While raising three biological children, I met young adults who had meals at our home, joined us on vacations, and became a part of our family. Spending time with these kids allowed me to know them better. Angela became a part of our family after her first season of flag football at Aptos Junior High. When she returned to Aptos after college, I saw that she was looking for something to do to give her purpose. I first recruited her to coach throwers at the junior high and saw that she had a natural ability to connect with the athletes. When I was offered the head coaching position of the inaugural girls flag football team at Aptos High School, I asked Angela to join me as one of the coaches.

In a 2023 commencement speech at Smith's College, Reshma Saujani speaks of the birth of imposter syndrome, a tool to "hold women back." Angela mentions her imposter syndrome as a flag football coach in her interview. Being brave requires finding the courage to do things for which you have self-doubt and lack confidence. Angela was courageous on her journey, serving as a role model for these young adults.

Be brave. Do hard things. Believe.

Angela described "imposter syndrome" as the hardest part of coaching. She asked herself, "Do I belong here? Do I know what I am doing? Will I let these girls and Coach Russo down?" Trying something new was challenging and terrifying for her, but she did it, and from this experience, she learned she could do hard things.

Coach Gabriella (Gabbie) Russo

- Position: Specialty Position Coordinator
- Seasons Coached Flag Football: 1
- Seasons Played Flag Football: 4
- Positions Played: Rush, Center
- Other Sports Played: Soccer, Basketball (including one year in college)
- Three Words That Describe Gabriella: Fun, Confident, Thoughtful

While I was growing up, I watched my older and younger brothers play flag football on their teams coached by my dad. Sometimes, I would go to practice, catch footballs, chase down players, and try to pull their flags. I didn't know any girls in the league, so I played basketball and soccer but never flag football. That changed when I got to junior high, where I played GFF on the school team and then in the local league as the only all-girl team against teams who were all boys.

I didn't plan to coach. My full-time job made attending all of the practices challenging. But one summer day, I decided to join my mom, who was coaching the Aptos High School Girls' Flag Football team. It was so much fun that I joined the coaching staff.

It's exciting that girls and women now have another opportunity to be involved in sports. Every sport has differences in the technical application of skills needed to play the game. However, flag football skills can be easily applied to these sports. The footwork used in GFF is the same as any sport that requires sharp cuts and agility. Ellie, a track and field team thrower, even said about using your hip when practicing passing one day, "Oh, like how we throw a shot put." When our GFF season ended, we'd watch our athletes play their other sports and see their GFF skills used on the court and field. The energy from our team was so exciting. I'd encourage anyone interested in playing GFF for their school to do it!

Players' Audible

Coach Gabbie has made me realize that it is okay to be a strong, confident woman in this world. She uses her voice to advocate and to speak her mind, and that's something I have always been shamed for doing. Like many other girls, I have been called bossy instead of acknowledged as a leader. Coach Gabbie role models confidence in herself and what she believes. (Mia P)

The dynamic between Coach Gabbie and me seems like we have known each other for a long time. She is our thoughtful coach who always remembers to bring extra water bottles and snacks to take care of the players. She also has fun with us, which helps us feel comfortable with each other. (Ellie)

Coach Denise

Raising a human to be confident in the world is a journey itself. But, raising a confident child to be a confident woman in the world has an extra set of challenges, including an opportunity to practice peaceful navigation of a meaningful relationship. You must learn when to request vs demand and when to plant seeds and then sit back and wait. Knowing my daughter had some schedule conflicts, I didn't specifically ask if she wanted to coach with me. At home, however, I frequently (OK, obsessively) talked about our practices. When Gabriella asked if she could coach with us, I was thrilled. I knew she'd be an asset to the team! Gabriella brought the experience of not only being a multi-sport athlete but also an understanding of what it means to play a team sport at the collegiate level. Her suggestions for managing practices and game substitutions of a large group of players (28 for a sport that fields 7) were instrumental to our success. College coaches often recruit multi-sport high school players because they are "more well rounded, have a diversity of skill sets, and increased athletic IQ and instincts" (Ohanian, 2023). Gabriella took advantage of opportunities for developing flag football skills that cross over into the other sports of our athletes.

Be brave. Do hard things. Believe.

Gabriella reflected that playing football <a new sport to most> is a chance to be bold and try something new. Each game, win or lose, provides opportunities to continue to improve. This is something you can do at any crossroads in life and at times when you need courage and motivation. This is a life skill that benefits everyone on the team.

Coach Gabby Fely

- Position: Assistant Coach
- Seasons Coached Flag Football: 3
- Seasons Played Flag Football: 2
- Position Played: Rush, Center
- Other Sports Played: Soccer (Junior High)
- Three Words That Describe Gabby: Friendly, Entertaining, Supportive

I met Denise when I played soccer in 7th grade at the junior high. When she encouraged me to try out for the school's girls flag football team, I did. During that flag football season, I played on a team with my friends and learned a new sport. Years later, Denise asked me to join her on that field again as a coach. In my second season of coaching at junior high, GFF became the newest sanctioned varsity sport in the high school. I didn't think I had enough experience to coach at the high school, but I knew I worked well with Denise, so when she asked me to join, I excitedly agreed.

Coaching a high school varsity team was intimidating, on a whole different level than the junior high. We were making history (or HERstory, as Denise says). Junior high school GFF was about learning and having fun, with winning a bonus. At the high school, we were building a new program from the ground up to be competitive. We had to be firmer as coaches, and there was more pressure to perform well. There was also a lot of confusion about the rules, which was frustrating because a wrong call made by not knowing the rules could (and did) cost us a game.

34

The confusion around the rules motivated me to be firm by ensuring the referees had a copy to review.

It is important for the players to have GFF as it is a safer option for girls to play football. It opens another door for females to participate in sports. I didn't have the option to play GFF in high school. So, being a part of this was special. The high level of school spirit at the homecoming game was exciting. Team bonding activities were also entertaining. At the end of our final game, I had to tell the girls I wouldn't be able to come back the next season so that I could focus on my college classes. It was bittersweet, having just become the first undefeated league champions in SCCAL history but knowing we wouldn't share the same connection next season.

Players' Audible

Coach Gabby was like a sister. She was easy to talk to if I needed help with anything. I'm glad she was my coach last year, and I will miss having her around in our second season. (Ellie)

Coach Gabby's ability to command respect at a young age inspired me to embrace my role as a player. (Madi P)

Coach Denise

As a multi-sport coach at the junior high, I have interacted with many athletes over the years. Over time, I often lose track of them. Sometimes, our paths cross at the local community college where I am an associate faculty member. When Gabby came into my classroom, I remembered her as one of the wing players on my soccer team who was small but mighty and as one of my fast flag football players. I was looking for someone to help me coach at the junior high, and after observing her leadership skills in my team-based classroom, I convincingly persuaded her to join me for GFF.

Gabby was the youngest coach on our staff, still in college when we started coaching together. That made her extra relatable to our players, being able to talk to someone on the path most of them would follow after high school graduation. We all felt that coaching varsity has a different intensity than junior high. But Gabby remained mellow most of the time, except when not everyone knew the rules or when we felt unheard as coaches. The players felt connected to her, which was beneficial for our team dynamic of community and collaboration.

Be brave. Do hard things. Believe.

Gabby found it hard to adjust to the intensity of coaching that matched a varsity-level team. "I was used to the Jr. High where it was all about celebrating the learning and just having fun with it." Not that far removed from high school herself, she had to learn to manage the pressure of coaching a high school sport. Although we still had fun, we were now calling plays and defenses with an intention to win. She said we all had to be brave to join this first team, but with a lot of hard work and patience, it paid off. Gabby's final words after having been brave were, "I am proud to have been a part of this program."

Third Quarter: The Players

36

Alexa

- Positions: MB, Receiver
- Class: Senior
- Previous Seasons Played Flag Football: 0
- Other Sports Played: Volleyball, Track and Field
- Three Words That Describe Alexa: Brave, Supportive, Adaptable

I have always loved tackle football but thought that flag football looked fun to play as a great alternative to the contact sport of tackle football. It was an enjoyable way to be active while learning a new sport. It was different from my usual sport of volleyball. One notable thing was the speed of the game. In GFF, there is a running clock, and you have to hustle to get your next play off before the time expires. The afternoon conditioning sessions were hard. I am glad I played because I enjoyed it so much and just wish I had the opportunity for more than one season.

My favorite memories involved team bonding. Those activities made the team special, whether a movie night or team dinner. I also really enjoyed the day we went swimming after having done some intense conditioning. I loved getting to know everyone and being able to learn a new sport without the feeling of being judged. It was a space where we could learn and make mistakes. I also enjoyed how connected and accepting the team was of each other. It was a privilege to play a sport I had never done before, and it came with so many amazing people along the way. While my time playing was short, I enjoyed every second of it.

Being a part of a team that made history in a new sport was meaningful. While I have always loved football, I wasn't willing to put my body on the line playing tackle football. Injuries still happen, even in non-contact sports, but flag football offers a better option, especially for girls who don't want to play tackle football against boys. It meant a lot to be a part of a team making sports history by giving girls another option to play for their high school.

Coach Denise

Alexa joined our team as a novice flag football player. Although she has many friends and is well-liked, she came out for flag football to experience something new. She was easygoing and friendly and made everyone comfortable, especially our underclass students. That didn't stop her from being aggressive on defense and an effective flag-puller.

Early in our season, Alexa sustained an ACL injury, ending her playtime for the season. But, even from the sideline, she encouraged and supported her team to be their best. One of my favorite memories was having her snap the ball with a brace on her leg at our Senior Night game. Injuries happen in any sport, but what an athlete does after that, their attitude and ongoing commitment to their teammates is a true look at their character.

Be brave. Do hard things. Believe.

Alexa described a situation where our players had to be brave, and other players mentioned it in their interviews. Sometimes, people are still learning the rules on the field in a new sport. In our first game, we experienced this and what it felt like. Our team had to keep playing. We went on to lose that game, but our team learned how to persevere in this type of hard situation.

Angelique

- Positions: Wide Receiver, Safety
- All League: 2nd Team
- Class: Senior
- Previous Seasons Played Flag Football: 1
- Other Sports Played: Soccer, Beach Volleyball
- Three Words That Describe Angelique: Athletic, Sure-handed, Moxie

My father taught me at a young age how to catch a football. I have always loved the sport and had even considered playing tackle with the boys. (The varsity tackle team did have one girl on their team, but most years, it is only boys.) I was excited to play when I heard that GFF was an option, even though it meant balancing that with my comp soccer team.

Playing both sports on the same day sometimes was a challenge. I could definitely feel how tired that made me. But playing two sports helped my athleticism. I became faster and stronger from being a multisport athlete. For GFF, I was initially a wide receiver. I loved catching the ball, but I also learned the importance of running my routes correctly so that someone else would be open to advance the ball.

My favorite memory from GFF was during our senior night game. I had been playing more defense as a safety. That night, I had three interceptions that helped our team win our final home game. I felt inspired by the people I was with, who encouraged and supported my playing GFF. Playing flag football gives us girl power. Together, we played a non-contact version of a sport usually only played by boys. As a team of flag football players, we learned from our losses and strengthened ourselves physically and mentally.

Coach Denise

According to Merriam-Webster's dictionary, moxie means "courage, determination." That was the word I was looking for when thinking of how to describe Angelique. When I met her when she was in 8th grade, I could just tell she was going to be an aggressive player on the offense. That season was cut short during the pandemic, and I missed seeing what this player could do on a football field. When she came out as a senior in high school, I was finally allowed to see this moxie.

At the high school, we negotiated which side of the ball Angelique should play. She has the speed and hands to be an excellent wide receiver. But as our season progressed and our opponents became more accurate with their long balls, we adjusted to have her defend the long ball. That allowed us to see how fierce of a competitor Angelique truly is. I cannot forget the vision of her coming down with the ball out of the hands of three opposing players. Angelique ended up leading the team in interceptions and pick-6s.

Be brave. Do hard things. Believe.

Angelique described the challenge of trying something new as hard. She encourages pushing yourself to become stronger and more confident. "You can only get better from trusting that you can keep going even when it gets hard."

Annika

- Position: Wide Receiver, Middle Back, Corner
- Class: Sophomore
- Previous Seasons Played Flag Football: 0
- Other Sports Played: Lacrosse
- Three Words That Describe Annika: Patient, Reliable, Cheerful

I thought it would be fun to try flag football with one of my friends. I had two years of experience as a lacrosse player, including a year on the first girls vs. coed team. My experience in lacrosse helped me as we got started with flag football. Lacrosse was more physical, with constant running which differs from the stop-and-go of running plays in GFF. I had a concussion early in the season which set me behind in learning the skills at the level of my teammates. But with the support of my team and by working hard at practice, I was able to catch up.

What I loved about playing GFF was the people I met on the team. Beyond being teammates, I made many good friends, which added to the season's enjoyment. It was already exciting to be a part of an inaugural team. But what I loved the most were the relationships we created. We always cheered each other on in each game. And no matter how well we played, we supported each other. I really enjoyed being a part of this team.

It was cool to be able to play this new sport. We had several games where our skills were close to our competitors'. These games were extra fun to play and fulfilling. It is important for girls to have opportunities to play sports.

Introducing GFF provides girls another chance to be student-athletes and creates an opportunity to play a sport in the future.

Coach Denise

We first met Annika at "tryouts" in the Fall. She had just participated on our school's first Girls Lacrosse team and was motivated to try another new sport with her friend. Early in our season, a bike-related concussion sidelined her from practices. During this time, Annika was missing time devoted to essential skills development. For some athletes, this would be a deterrent from continuing with the sport. But we were thrilled that Annika returned after her healthcare team cleared her. She impressed us with her commitment to catching up with her peers.

Be brave. Do hard things. Believe.

Learning something new is hard according to Anika. That does not deter her though as she set to learning two new sports in high school. She encourages people to keep trying new things. If you believe in yourself and your team, it is worth the experience.

Ashlyn

- Position: Middle back
- Class: Freshman
- Previous Seasons Played Flag Football: 0
- Other Sports Played: Lacrosse
- Three Words That Describe Ashlyn: Sweet, Committed, Hard-Working

Joining flag football was not easy for me. I wasn't just trying a new sport; I was also starting a new public high school after attending a small private school. When I first arrived in the summer, I didn't know many people. But soon, I was enjoying scrimmages and games with my teammates. We also had fun off the field. Team bonding included dinners and playing games at our coach's house. On birthdays, we'd sing to the birthday player while they ran down the field, and then we'd chase them, which ended in a group birthday hug once we caught them. Playing flag football has been the best experience of my life. My teammates are hard-working and supportive, and I look forward to another season.

Knowing that this was the first year of girls' flag football in California high schools made me excited about making a difference in girls' sports. Whether we won or lost did not matter. The experience alone was exciting. Most high school sports have boys' and girls' teams, but football never did until now. Before, even if a girl wanted to play football, she may not have wanted to play tackle football. And even though they aren't technically the same sport, now that flag football is an option, it gives girls a chance to try something new. GFF provides an opportunity for girls to feel equal and to play with a football like boys do. It was hard to juggle homework, family, practices, and being a first-time student in a large public school, but I am grateful to be a part of something big with a great group of girls and fantastic coaches.

Coach Denise

You know those people who just seem to bring positivity to everything they do, as if the sun gets a little brighter when they show up? That is Ashlyn. She came out for summer, new to the school district, knowing very few people in attendance. She was a little quiet and reserved but always smiling and positive. At first, she stood off to the side with the one other friend who came to flag football with her. But, before we knew it, we couldn't distinguish between long-time friends or friendships made on the team. I remember being on campus for something during the season, and seeing Ashlyn, surrounded by some of these football friends, enjoying her day. I believe her time on the team fostered the building of these new relationships.

In her interview, Ashlyn describes her teammates as hard-working, a quality she emulates. She'd concentrate on the directions for each skill and then go out and execute. She became one of the best players at running without flag guarding (a flag football penalty in which the offensive player uses their hand to prevent the defense from pulling their flag). One day, when running a tricky zone-defense drill, it just clicked for her. I celebrated with a loud "YES!" and could see her pride in learning the new skill. Her work ethic extended beyond the season, as well. She was a committed participant in off-season strength and conditioning. She focused on developing balance, strength, and speed and always wanted to do a little more to get even better. If she made a mistake, she would laugh about it, come back, and try even harder next time.

Be brave. Do hard things. Believe.

"I struggle with performance anxiety and lack self-confidence" says Ashlyn. Trying something new was not easy. She knew if she was going to continue, she would need to believe in herself. She found the pep talks and pregame inspirational quotes before the games helped her confidence improve. This improvement of her believing in herself was noticeable to all of us and transferred into her trying out for lacrosse in the spring.

Ava (Gavin)

- Position: Running back, Safety
- Class: Senior
- Previous Seasons Played Flag Football: 1
- Other Sports Played: Soccer, Track
- Three Words That Describe Ava: Speedy, Engaging, Intelligent

I decided to play flag football because I had played for Coach Denise in junior high, and I loved her and knew it would be a lot of fun. I was also looking for a fall sport to keep me in shape for soccer and track. Flag football did keep me in shape for my other sports. But it did more than that. Not only did my speed improve, but my critical thinking and field skills increased, which helped me become a better soccer player this year.

Playing in this inaugural season meant we were #makingherstory. Flag football is a fun sport that everyone should try playing. But more than that, it expands the horizon of sports opportunities, from recreation to high school to college. It gives girls another opportunity to be included in sports. It provides for more equal representation in sports for girls and women.

Aside from the fun of playing, flag football provides a chance to meet new people and to be part of a team. I loved celebrating our successes with each other and dancing to the music during warmups at practice. I made a lot of new friends, including meeting Mary, who is now my best friend. Playing a new sport was difficult at first, but the coaches did a great job of helping us to understand the game. I will never forget how I felt when I got my first touchdown or how rewarding it was to be undefeated in the league.

Coach Denise

When Ava came out for flag football at the junior high, I negotiated to have her play on defense. In addition to appreciating her sense of humor, wearing a shirt with the name "Gavin" on it, which she adopted as her flag football persona, she was a skilled athlete. But, when she showcased her speed and ability to run the ball, I had to concede to allow her to play primarily on the offensive side of the ball. At the junior high, she honed her skill for advancing the ball and scoring touchdowns. Building on this success, Ava was second in rushing yards and TDs in our high school season, defining her success as an offensive player.

Her success didn't end there. It's the last two minutes of the high school season's final game. The result of this game would keep us on the road to being undefeated in the league. A personnel change by the coaches results in 6 defensive players (not 7) on the field. The opponents run the ball. Ava misses the flag on her first attempt, and the running back is headed to the end zone. But Ava doesn't give up and continues to chase the running back, ultimately pulling the flag and stopping what might have been a game-changing TD. In this play where she prevented the opponent from scoring a that TD, Ava showcased her important contribution on both sides of the ball.

Be brave. Do hard things. Believe.

Ava reports that learning the routes and plays took a lot of work. The stop-and-go of running plays is unique for a soccer player. She said that at first, it was hard, but eventually, with the support of coaches and teammates, it became easier. Trying new things is scary but worth it. Ava tells anyone considering flag football that it is the most fun sport out there, and they should play. We want to add if you want to take on an alter-ego for flag football, that can be extra fun, too!

Dakota

- Position: QB
- Class: Freshman
- Previous Seasons Played Flag Football: 1
- Other Sports Played: Basketball, Track and Field
- Three Words That Describe Dakota: Focused, Determined, Introspective

While we were playing junior high football, we were told that GFF would be available to us at the high school in our freshman year. I loved playing in junior high and looked forward to the opportunity to develop my skills and improve. It opened up a whole new amazing phase of my life. Playing flag football also helped me get stronger and faster for my other sports.

Playing flag football makes me feel like I can do anything. It isn't just boys who can play football anymore. Flag football is an up-and-coming sport that is growing worldwide. (It will be an Olympic sport in 2028.) It is important for girls to have a similar option for this sport. Having this sport available to girls shows the progress that we are making for women in sports.

I loved all the team bonding activities in which we participated to bring us all together. We had beach nights and movie nights and dinners, and they were all so fun. There were hard moments, like having to be patient while getting through an injury. But my team was there for me. I am grateful for the comradery that we have as we look forward to playing next season.

Coach Denise

It truly was a joy to watch players that I met while coaching at the junior high continue their friendships into the high school as GFF teammates. There is an age gap between players, particularly the freshmen when compared to the seniors. The freshmen group grew particularly close with one another, continuing these friendships off the field. Even though certain age groups spent more time together, this diverse group of players grew together as one team who supported each other, especially when doing hard things.

Dakota's determination to learn the position of quarterback is remarkable. She asks questions, works hard to implement, and is completely engaged in her sport. She knows the intensity of this position from both the physical and emotional perspective. Dakota asks for input and then practices implementing the coaching advice. Her self-insight is commendable.

Be brave. Do hard things. Believe.

Being a quarterback can be a lot of pressure. In one of our games, we ended up in overtime, tied at the end of regulation playing time. Dakota reported being very nervous about playing in that game. Dakota's dad talked to her at the break and helped her to calm down. When she went back into the game, she threw the game winning touchdown pass. According to Dakota, being a part of GFF helps players to see themselves as strong woman, capable of anything.

Elenah

- Position: Corner
- Class: Sophomore
- Previous Seasons Played Flag Football: 3
- Other Sports Played: Martial Arts
- Three Words that Describe Elenah: Quick, Tenacious, Fierce

When I heard that flag football was being offered at the high school, I was excited. I played all three years in middle school and looked forward to continuing with the only team sport that I play. I already loved this sport but being able to represent our school in the first season that the GFF became an official high school sport in California was special.

This sport is different from my usual sport which is martial arts. In martial arts, the focus is on individual power and technique, with the outcome based solely on myself. With GFF, the focus is on the team. We use our skills to benefit how we play. Without working together, the game cannot happen. At practices, we work hard at our skills and drills to improve our agility and endurance and to build strength to help prevent injuries. We also must work hard to memorize plays. In both sports, you have to work hard at practice to make progress but in flag football that work needs to be done together.

Beyond playing the game, I really enjoyed being a part of a team. Relying on others was new to me. But I created many memories at our team bonding activities at Coach Denise's house or when celebrating birthdays by chasing the birthday player down. It also felt inclusive and special for girls to be able to play flag football. Although it has differences from tackle football, some of the skills and strategy are the same. It meant a lot to me to represent high school girls playing flag football.

Coach Denise

One of the first drills I run with my team is a flag pulling vice drill. I give a brief overview of how to perform it with instruction on flag pulling technique and then set them to work. This allows the coaching staff an opportunity to assess agility, speed, and coachability. The person in the offensive position steps and says their name. I then repeat their name back and on my "ready, hit" everyone runs the drill with the offensive player trying to escape from the flag pullers. Elenah had already gone through the drill and now it was her turn to pull flags. Almost as soon as I said, "ready, hit," she was on the right hip and of the offensive player, pulling her flag. I looked at her and said, "What's your name again?" She repeated it but I didn't think I recognized her as a player I had coached at the junior high. So, I asked, "Did you play for me at the junior high?" She grinned at me with a sparkle in her eye and said, "I played for a different school. We played against you."

Elenah was committed to continuing with her strength as a defensive player. Although many players get playing time on both sides of the ball, she was one of my players who was a defensive specialist. She is aggressive and quick and continues to work on protecting that sideline and stopping the other team's touchdown. She is not afraid to ask me how to improve. I look forward to watching her continue to improve.

Be Brave. Do hard things. Believe.

Playing flag football in high school was intimidating. Players like Elenah said that they worried about whether they would be good enough. Elenah's approach was to focus on being in the moment and taking small steps to improve. When asked about being brave and doing hard things, she discussed our first game (as many players did), where we saw how one play can impact the outcome. She said that this is when she learned how working together as a team, and helping each other, gives players the support that they need to not to be afraid.

Ellie

- Position: Safety, Running Back
- Class: Freshman
- Previous Seasons Played Flag Football: 2
- Other Sports Played: Track and Field (thrower)
- Three Words That Describe Ellie: Committed, Speedy, Competitive

Track and field has been my primary sport for a long time. For fun, I played flag football at the junior high. When I found out that GFF was going to be offered as a new sport at the high school with the same coaches, I decided I'd try it out. Balancing throws practice and homework with a varsity practice was a challenge. But participating in a new sport gave me the chance to practice and develop other skills.

Playing GFF as a freshman was a great way to start my high school career. It was a great way to meet people as a new high school student. I love the people that I met on my team. They helped me to be comfortable in my new school environment and were why it was such an enjoyable experience. It wasn't easy being the first season of a new sport. People didn't really understand it at first, a new game, new skills to develop, new rules to learn. But being a part of the first flag football team was pretty amazing. As flag football continues to grow, girls and women will have more opportunities to participate in sport.

Coach Denise

Ellie has a focus and determination as an athlete that cannot be missed. During the flag football season, she still made time to work with her throws coach. In the off-season, she was a committed participant in strength and conditioning. In the spring, she not only hit her PR (personal record) in shot put and discus, but she was also a part of the varsity throws team as a freshman and one of a few athletes on her team to qualify for CCS semi-finals.

Since Ellie is a strong thrower, it seemed that quarterback would be the likely place for her. After working with her briefly, two things became very apparent. In our league where a quarterback is limited in how often they can take the (run) option, her speed would be wasted at QB. Also, she instinctively could read a quarterback and quickly play defense against the offensive player in her position at safety. Having her start at defense was the right choice as she tied for most flag pulls (tackles) in the season. In addition to her success on varsity in track, she was a starting varsity GFF player as a freshman.

Be brave. Do hard things. Believe.

It was in a game that was one of only two losses for the varsity players that we really saw our players become brave. In the first half of the game, our players were tentative on the field, seemingly a little scared by the size and aggressiveness of our opponents. At half time, we discussed their apprehension and modified our game plan. The players had to believe in themselves and continue to play which seemed like a hard thing. Ellie described, "One specific game I am proud of is the Monterey game. Although we lost this game, I was proud of our team for how we didn't give up." The team bravely adjusted in the second half that they were able to build on for the rest of the season.

Emi

- Position: Middle Back, Running Back (All)
- Class: Freshman
- Previous Seasons Played Flag Football: 4
- Other Sports Played: Basketball
- Three Words That Describe Emi: Tenacious, Fearless, Versatile

I wanted to play flag football in high school because I didn't want to lose the sport I had been playing and practicing for so long. I began playing flag football at a younger age, but when I came to high school, I decided to play basketball as my primary sport. I was scared for a long time that I would have to quit playing flag football when I got into high school, but when I saw that I could keep playing, I came out for the team.

Playing GFF in the Fall helped me with my strength, footwork, and speed, which are important in many sports, including basketball. Although playing GFF helped me prepare for basketball, the sports have some significant differences. In GFF, the defense and offense are separate, with breaks between plays used to strategize your next move. Basketball is a constant back-and-forth game with minimal breaks, and it can sometimes become incredibly physical. Playing both sports helps me prepare for the other.

Being a part of this team was special as we made history. We were a part of the next steps forward in the future of girls who want to play sports. Girls who wanted to play football but never got the chance now have that opportunity. This is incredibly important because football in our country is very visible, and having an option for girls is a huge step forward. Flag football is an amazing sport, and I would tell anyone interested in playing that it can help develop athletic abilities. Win or lose, I enjoyed playing in the games as we learned from each one. And our athletic skills improved.

Beyond that, GFF provided an opportunity to make new and stronger friendships. GFF is like a second home to me, and it seems to be the same for my teammates. Being a part of the team wasn't just about the sport but also our impact on each other. My favorite memories are from our team bondings at Coach Denise's house and our late practices and games where we would have fun and laugh with one another. I enjoyed being outside with my friends, learning, laughing, and exercising together, enjoying the community and friendships we made.

Coach Denise

Do you know what a utility player is? This is an athlete that you can literally put into every position. Emi was that player on our team. She just has football sense. She can see a hole, find an open receiver, and chase down almost any player when on defense. When she didn't show up for summer practice, focusing on basketball, I was....what is the word when you are simultaneously happy and disappointed? Bittersweet, that is what I felt. I was happy that she was pursuing her primary sport but knew it was a loss of both an athlete and a tremendous team player for GFF.

Emi wasn't the only player who had to make difficult decisions about the sport they would play. When GFF was first announced at the high school, over 70 girls were interested in playing. Other school and competitive rec league sports became a barrier for many who had to make hard decisions. Those who couldn't commit to our varsity schedule were not a part of our team. But those who adjusted their schedules benefitted. In the article "Why College Coaches Prefer Multi-Sport Athletes," coaches describe how multi-sport high school athletes improve their sports IQ and game instincts and diversify their skills, making them more athletic players. We were grateful for our players, like Emi, who committed and contributed to our team.

Be brave. Do hard things. Believe.

Sometimes, games can be challenging. We had quite a few that were this first year as built a program and learned to play at a varsity level. Emi reflected that it may seem easy to quit, but by pushing yourself through these difficult times, that is when you learn to play your best.

Gaby

- Position: QB
- League Awards: All League 1st Team QB
- Class: Junior
- Previous Seasons Played Flag Football: ½ (interrupted by COVID-19 Shelter in Place)
- Other Sports Played: Soccer
- Three Words That Describe Gaby: Poised, Calm, Collected

I loved playing flag football in junior high, but our season was cut short due to COVID-19. When football was offered as an option in high school, I was excited to play again, this time at a higher level of play and in the first year of being a high school varsity sport. That meant more than I can put into words, and it will mean more and more to me as time goes on and more teams experience what I have been a part of in this inaugural year. I can't wait for the day that I get to see GFF on the same level as other sports.

Like many parts of society, football has been a male-dominated sport forever. Girls' Flag Football (GFF) offers women a new sport and an opportunity to perform in a space exclusive to them. Most sports have a female counterpart to the male sport, but football is usually exclusively for men. GFF gives women a chance to shine without being compared to the performance of a male and gives them something to call their own.

Flag football created a community that I loved. I had stopped playing school soccer and missed being a high school athlete. I do not usually go out of my way to befriend people, especially at school. But, by joining the flag football team, I met people with similar interests that I enjoy being around. I developed and improved my skills alongside my teammates and connected with new friends. I'd encourage anyone to play. You will grow as a person and an athlete. I am excited to be a part of a group spreading the message about what this sport offers to young athletes!

Game time was my favorite part of the season! I enjoyed watching my teammates adapt to the teams we played, gaining more confidence as the game progressed. I loved the rush when the game-ending whistle was blown, signaling we had won. Winning the end-of-season tournament was a highlight as well. It was great coming out on top of so many amazing teams. And although it was challenging at first, I found joy in carrying the control and responsibility that my position brings. One mistake can cost the team the entire game, making winning more rewarding.

We faced some challenges this season. As a new sport, the rules were evolving, and coaches and referees had varying interpretations. Occasionally, it affected the outcome of the game, which was hard to accept. In one game, one call changed the game's momentum in a devastating and chaotic way. I felt responsible for the resulting loss. However, I took that opportunity to learn to forgive myself. Some decisions are out of my control, and I must accept them without letting them phase me. My coaches recognized this, and I now perform better under pressure.

Coach Denise

A quarterback's success often depends on their patience when reading the field while pressured by a defensive player rushing at them (running at them attempting to pull their flags before the QB can pass the ball). But Gaby is as calm, cool, and collected in the pocket as she is when walking on the field in her sunglasses. Adding to her threat at quarterback is her speed on the run. She will gain yards by sprinting up the field if she doesn't see an open receiver. Most important is her gift of shaking off a bad play and focusing on the next one. To be successful in this position, you need a memory that is as short as Dory's.

The game that Gaby described, where she felt responsible for the loss, rattled many of our players (others mention it in their story's, as well). It also created a high level of self-doubt for me that led me to thinking I wasn't up to the task of coaching a varsity team. But in these experiences, I grew with my players. After one, ok actually three, nights of sleep lost to self-doubt, I turned the corner and truly stepped into my role of "head coach." This loss on the field turned into a psychological win for the team as we processed how to improve. I looked at Gaby and quoted, "You know what the happiest animal in the world is? It's a goldfish. It's got a 10-second memory. Be a goldfish." (Ted Lasso). With a call that changed the outcome of this game, Gaby leaned into her sunglass-wearing poise and metamorphosed into "The Goldfish."

Be brave. Do hard things. Believe.

"My ability to be "the goldfish" - unphased by tough situations and keeping my head up no matter the circumstances - reflects the idea of being brave, doing hard things, and believing," said Gaby. When the other team had an amazing defense, Gaby described how it was hard to remain as positive as she would be against an easier opponent. When she saw her receiver open deep, it was challenging to choose to make the deep pass to them. Sometime of these deep passes resulted in an interception. This might make some QBs not want to make these long passes anymore. But by believing in herself, she could shake this off and attempt the deep pass the next time a receiver was open.

Izzy: Captain

- Position: RB, Corner
- All League: 1st Team Offensive Player; MVP
- Team Award: Anchor
- Class: Junior
- Previous Seasons Played Flag Football: ½ (interrupted by COVID-19 Shelter in Place)
- Other Sports Played: Soccer, Track
- Three Words About Izzy: Intentional, Inspirational, Competitive

My interest in playing flag football was sparked by the opportunity to break barriers for female athletes. Being given an opportunity to showcase our skills, passion, and determination with a football, which usually only happens for male athletes, was a historic moment for us. Flag football empowers girls to embrace athleticism, teamwork, and competition in a traditionally male-dominated space. It sends a positive message that girls are just as capable and deserving of opportunities in sports as boys and is a step towards a more inclusive and equitable society. As our coach said, we were making "herstory," paving the way for future generations of female athletes.

This experience was incredibly rewarding for me. It was an honor to be a captain on our team. I loved the competitive aspect of learning a new sport. I cared a lot, maybe too much, about working with my teammates to lead us to a memorable and successful inaugural season. A highlight of this season was scoring the first-ever touchdown in the Central Coast Section (CCS). This TD happened in the first CCS game, which we were close to winning. However, there was some confusion about the rules, and a call made at the end of the game caused us to turn over the ball. This turnover gave our opponent one last chance to score, and they capitalized on that to win the game. Although this was very upsetting, I learned how to speak up as a captain, which made me more confident in my other sports.

In a different game, we came in as the underdogs. Doing the extra work at practice, our entire team stepped up to the challenge. It was obvious that this sport is all about teamwork. We had to believe in ourselves. We worked hard to learn together. We celebrated our individual and shared moments of success. We cried when it ended. Some of my favorite memories were found in the new friends I made and in celebrating each other together. The bonds formed and the unwavering support we gave each other made this year unforgettable.

Coach Denise

When I first met her at junior high soccer tryouts, I encouraged her to be more aggressive if she wanted to make the team. I don't remember this, but she does! I cannot imagine a team where Izzy would have tried out for me that she wouldn't have made. The pandemic cut short my opportunity to coach her in flag football. When students were allowed back to school a year later, we offered after-school "cohorts" for just a few sports (flag football wasn't included). Izzy came out for a soccer cohort which I coached and emerged as a leader of that group. When we met again at flag football at the high school, she was the obvious choice for the one coach-selected team captain.

In her interview, Izzy mentioned a game that came up a lot in player interviews. It was game-changing as we were in the lead and set to run the clock out with the W. The call, the confusion, and the emotion resulted in a breakdown in our performance in those final two minutes.

This was a huge learning opportunity for our team to respect the referee's decision and keep our heads in the game. Izzy took matters into her own hands, creating a Kahoot to test our knowledge of the rules. See what I mean? Definitely a leader. Izzy won the team "anchor" award for this type of leadership and overall commitment to her team.

Be brave. Do hard things. Believe.

Trying something new provides an opportunity to develop confidence. Playing flag football wasn't just about learning a new sport for athletes. According to Izzy, it was about challenging norms and creating a more inclusive future where every girl can confidently pursue her passions on the field and beyond. In this inaugural season, Izzy developed courage, perseverance, and the power of believing there's no limit to what we can achieve.

Janelle

- Position: Wide Receiver, Middle Back
- Class: Junior
- Previous Seasons Played Flag Football: 1
- Other Sports Played: Track and Field
- Three Words That Describe Janelle: Willing, Friendly, Introspective

Competing with a team was a new experience for me. I was a track and field sprinter and a long jumper, and in that sport participation is individual. I was excited to be a part of a new sport where I would rely on other people while we were competing. Having to rely on other people this way was a nice feeling. Because it was a new sport for many of us, it lessened the fear I typically had with team sports. I learned that working together as a team, you always have other people to back you up if anything goes wrong.

It took getting used to the fact that this wasn't just about me performing individually. But, once I got into the mentality of working together, I could see that this strengthened our team. Luckily, since the other players were so inclusive, getting into a team mindset was easy and happened quickly. I think our team was like no other. I would get nervous and find it hard to catch the ball, but that was okay as my team encouraged my efforts. Although we all got along from the start our bond grew stronger as we supported each other. Being a part of this team is what made playing GFF most enjoyable.

Playing flag football felt like a way to start change, not only for my school to gain a new sport but for all women who wish to play flag football and for the overall future of professional sports. Sports, in general, already lack the presence of women, so what better way to promote women's sports than to introduce a new one that will attract more women to get involved? Offering GFF helps make up for the lack of women in sports. And it is an additional way for women to find and express themselves and grow. We lost our first game, which became an opportunity for us to learn to identify our weaknesses and build a stronger team. This opportunity motivated me to try my best so my team could show how much women can accomplish if we're just given the chance.

Coach Denise

Janelle showed up to our team with minimal experience in team play. She wasn't used to her performance being intricately linked with others. Drawing on my experience as an equestrian, I think there is a different pressure between competing individually vs on a team. In individual competition a mistake may affect your personal outcome, but it doesn't generally change the outcome for a group of people. In a team sport, one mistake can feel like the difference between a win and a loss. (To be fair, the end result is based on what happened during the full game and not just one play.) There is pressure that you may let your teammates down. Janelle stepped up to this new challenge. She was quiet and attentive, clearly listening to instructions and thinking through the execution. I always felt that she was mentally picturing our instructions before implementing them. Learning new skills is hard work, and she showed up every day, motivated to learn, growing her football skills, and quickly becoming a cohesive team member.

Watching the metamorphosis of a group of individuals in different grades, backgrounds, and sports experiences was one of the high points of coaching this team. When Janelle first joined our team, she was quiet and cautious, used to completing individually. But we had the opportunity to watch her come out of her shell, sharing her positive attitude and sense of humor. She quickly made new friends as she became a member of this group of people breaking gender barriers in this new sport. And she learned the power of having a solid group of girls as part of her team.

Be brave. Do hard things. Believe.

Janelle's response to this question was, "This quote is my whole experience with flag football in one sentence. That's my biggest takeaway from this experience. Since day one, I was terrified even to show my face to this new group of people, but once I did it and tried it out for myself, I found a new favorite sport." Janelle encourages anyone interested in playing flag football to just do it. She is excited that it offers an opportunity for freedom and joy with the potential to grow as a professional sport and as one of the newest Olympic sports.

Julia

- Position: Center, Middle Back
- Class: Sophomore
- Previous Seasons Played Flag Football: 2
- Other Sports Played: Track and Field
- Three Words That Describe Julia: Amusing, Energetic, Loyal

I came out for the GFF because I was excited to participate in a new sport. When I was younger, I tried other sports, but I never really stayed with one sport like most other kids did. In junior high, I found flag football. Our school had a team which I made both years I was there but there wasn't an option to keep playing after that. As a freshman, I continued with track since I couldn't play flag. That changed in my sophomore year, when GFF started at many of the high schools in California.

Playing on the inaugural flag football team was an exciting experience. Because it was a new sport in high school, most players were learning to play with little to no experience. And everyone was working to learn the rules. That made it hard, but it was worth it. Flag football is an amazing option for girls. It helps show society what we can do, that if a person wants to, they can achieve anything. Being a part of that and knowing we are starting something that can lead to greatness is a very cool feeling.

I am a thrower for the high school track and field team. But GFF was different. Girls flag football didn't feel like we were just focused on our individual practice or game participation. We had to learn to work together as a team. We became a family. I looked forward to our daily practices. My favorite memories were when we were all tired and exhausted after a long school day. But then we all came to practice, and quickly everyone's moods were boosted. We sang along to the music on the speaker, lived in the moment, and had a great time together.

Coach Denise

Like any varsity team, we had first-string players (those who started each game) and then a very deep bench (players who substitute for those starters). Twenty-eight players are a lot for a sport that fields seven, but in this first year, most schools only had a varsity team, even though we had enough for a Junior Varsity (JV). When we played other schools with many players, we split our large groups and played two games to give everyone more playing time. Despite our best efforts, there were games where not everyone got on the field. It would have been easy for unfriendly competition between players to occur. But instead, friendships formed, and players supported each other regardless of position or playing time. It was the magic of our team. They bonded through learning a new sport, building each other up, and cheering on each other's accomplishments.

Julia and Mia P emulate the building of friendships that came from bonding with our sport. Before this year, these two players, in different grades, didn't know each other. Through their season-long hard work, they forged a friendship that will be long-lasting. They were nicknamed "the Tweedles" because they were always together, always having fun, and always positively influencing their team. They reflect the community that can be built when we move past our differences and work together as a team.

Be brave. Do hard things. Believe.

Being a part of something new is an opportunity for people to jump out of their comfort zone which provides an opportunity to mature.

Julia found the experience of playing GFF life changing. She made new friends, and cultivated one of those lifetime friendships that are rare and fulfilling. She also found a team sport that felt like the right fit for her athleticism and skills. Players were brave when they were vulnerable to making friends while sharing tears, laughter and, as Julia noted, even a little bit of blood, all of which happened while they grew together as a team.

June

- Position: Safety
- Class: Freshman
- Previous Seasons Played Flag Football: 1
- Other Sports Played: Basketball
- Three Words That Describe June: Positive, Patient, Level-headed

Basketball is a sport I have played for many years, but I tried flag football in my last year at the junior high and had so much fun I decided to play at the high school. It was challenging to learn a new sport, but it was also a nice break to play something different. Basketball and flag football have a lot of skills that cross over. Teamwork, leadership, vision (of the field or court), agility, and sprinting are all similar and playing one, helps me get better for the other.

Unlike basketball, where you are constantly moving between offense and defense, flag football starts a play with teams on one side of the ball. (An interception can quickly change that.) I found a defensive position that was a great fit for me. But for offense, I was asked to try different positions. It isn't easy when you are moving from running back to wide receiver. I kept a positive mindset and watched my teammates while they played their positions and did my best to learn and get better.

As much as I love playing GFF, I really came out for the people on the team. During the season, we enjoyed many team bonding opportunities, like making lanyards, having potlucks, and watching movies. We developed a community that had us singing together on the sidelines and crying as we watched the highlight reel at the awards banquet. The camaraderie between us is what I appreciated the most.

Being a part of this team, the first at the high school, the titles we won, is a forever memory for me. But what is important about GFF is how it contributes to gender equity in sports. It gives anyone who wants a realistic chance to try football. Tackle football is a more aggressive form of the game. Although the tackle team is co-ed, very few girls play on the team. There is a stigma that tackle is for boys, and girls on the team aren't always accepted. Plus, when a girl is on the tackle team, they don't get much playing time. There is a concern for bodily injury since girls' bodies are often smaller than tackle football player bodies. Having GFF available gives me hope that we will continue to move towards more equity between boys and girls in the future.

Coach Denise

With a team of 28 on a field that plays 7, it is sometimes necessary to try players in different positions, looking for the right combination on both sides of the ball. June's experience in team sports provided her with skills that aligned with multiple positions on the GFF team. On offense, she would jump in at running back or wide receiver and even took reps at snapping the ball. On defense, she rushed and played in the middle. It was in the secondary that we finally recognized her ability to patiently watch the play unfold. It can be frustrating to be moved around and asked to learn so many positions. But June's positive attitude took over and she prevailed.

I think it was the sweet nature of the freshmen helping each other that drew them together during the season. Being a freshman on a team of juniors and seniors can be intimidating. Although friendships were made between players of all different grades, the freshmen group had a shared sense of skill and silliness that bonded them together. Many of them had the shared experience of having just played flag football at the junior high. But varsity flag football was different. They were asked to learn more and reminded to pay attention more frequently. And they were often playing against players who were older and had more physical development and sport experience. Staying positive in this environment was imperative to creating a cohesive team.

Be brave. Do hard things. Believe.

June shares how she didn't come out for the summer program before her freshman year started because she was timid and fearful of not knowing the girls or how to play well enough. When she came out for fall and met everyone, she questioned herself, "why didn't I participate in summer?" She realized she shouldn't have been afraid to try something new. Throughout the season, she was frequently asked to try a new position in a scrimmage or game that she hadn't practiced which is truly not easy. She learned to believe she could have new experiences and it would be OK. She said, "I realized that if you believe you can, you can."

Lauren

- Position: Rush, Wide Receiver
- Class: Freshman
- Previous Seasons Played Flag Football: 2
- Other Sports Played: Lacrosse
- Three Words That Describe Lauren: Quick, Quiet, Agile

I played flag football for two years in junior high. During my 8th grade season, it was announced that GFF was going to be a varsity sport at the high school. I enjoyed playing both years at my junior high, so I decided to join the team. It was challenging to manage the homework and varsity practice schedule, but worth it. I really enjoyed that playing on varsity helped me improve as a player.

Playing flag football was a way for me to meet new people and make friends. I appreciate team bonding activities like hosting a community bake sale and selling our treats even while it rained. I also enjoyed playing in games with my teammates. My favorite game was our homecoming game. Our opponents were strong, and we had to work hard as a team to win with the only touchdown scored in the game. It was exciting because we had a large crowd cheering us on.

Coach Denise

Lauren is the quietest player on our team. Even in our interview for this book, she used few words. Put her on the field though, and she makes a loud statement with her fast rush that forces a quarterback to make a quick and often wrong decision, helping our team earn deflections and interceptions. And, whenever she pulled two flags and I did my sideline jig, it earned me one of those shy grins, that suggested that either she thought my dance was funny or that she agreed with my own kids that I shouldn't dance in public.

Although Lauren doesn't say much with her words, her actions tell her story. Due to the large number of participants on our varsity team, we often split into two groups. In general, the teams were separated by grade level. Lauren was one of a few exceptions, grouped to play with the older students. Even just a few years of development at this age makes it challenging for younger players to be as quick, agile, and reactive as their older teammates. Lauren's focus and hard work during practice were key in her ongoing development at this level of play.

Be brave. Do hard things. Believe.

Playing with the older players when you are freshman isn't an easy task. Just by growth, development and experience, the older players tend to be stronger and faster. It often means less playing time in games, as well. Lauren never let this deter her, working hard at every practice to keep up with these older players. In fact, after playing flag football, she bravely went on to try lacrosse. We think that doing the hard work at GFF gave her the confidence to participate in this new team sport.

Maddie

- Position: Running Back, Middle Back
- Class: Senior
- Previous Seasons Played Flag Football: 0
- Other Sports Played: Basketball, Track, Soccer
- Three Words That Describe Maddie: Cheerful, Optimistic, Persevering

When Girls Flag Football was announced as a new sport, I was excited about making school history as part of the first team. Although I had done sports before, I hesitated to join teams where people with a history of playing together might be cliquey. In this space, GFF was relatively new to everyone. I came to summer practice with my best friend, who couldn't continue, and I was nervous about fitting in. However, teammates like Ellie reassured me when she told me, "Good job," and called me out to do the closing break, and I felt like I fit into this team. You could tell on this team that everyone wanted to be accepted, and they were.

Team bonding was an essential part of building friendships. I kept meeting new people of different ages and skills, and it was easy to make friends. It was exciting and fun. We wanted to win, and we often did win, but it never felt like we had to win or that winning was why we enjoyed it. We just appreciated each other. I would go to practices when I was tired or invited to other activities, and it was always worth it. Sometimes on teams, people don't want to help each other as they compete to be better than teammates and earn a starting position. But it wasn't like that on this team. We all wanted everyone to be the best they could be, and we supported each other without competing against each other. Even when we lost a game, we celebrated each other's interceptions, touchdowns, and successes.

What brought us together was this opportunity to play a version of football that girls don't usually play. It is intimidating and hard to get playing time in tackle football. Even though it was said that "Girls can play on a tackle team," and they can, GFF is a more legitimate and equitable opportunity to play football. I would never have played football if flag football wasn't an option. Now, I watch tackle football games, which I have never done before, and I understand the rules, the terms, and what is happening during the plays. Flag football has given girls more opportunities to understand football through the opportunity to play. Everyone deserves an equal opportunity to play every sport; GFF makes this possible.

Coach Denise

Maddie was the player on our team who would make us smile just by being around her. Her pervasive optimism is contagious. Maddie could have been overwhelmed as she took repetitions and played games in various positions, having to learn the different skills of multiple positions. But she rose to this difficult task, working hard to understand the nuances of each position and always with a willingness to learn! Each day, she came to practice with a positive attitude and as someone her teammates could rely on for support.

The positivity Maddie exemplified was contagious. Maddie's first touchdown came during a game where we had some sideline preparation problems (e.g., the coaches didn't have the play cards) that contributed to our loss. When the game was over, the players' response to Maddie's score was as great as if we had won. We cherish these moments of celebrating each other's success, no matter the game's final score.

Be brave. Do hard things. Believe.

Maddie was nervous about joining a sport alone once her best friend decided they couldn't participate. She thought it might be cliquey based on different people's skills. She describes that she was feeling too nervous to continue, but she made herself go anyway. Maddie describes that the players went from being strangers to putting ribbons in our hair before games, dancing, singing, and cheering each other's successes from the sidelines. "At Senior Night, I realized I had made these great friends from all grades, and I remember thinking, we did this," said Maddie. She reflects that she would have missed that if she had let her fears take over and hadn't joined the team.

Madi

- Position: Safety
- Class: Freshman
- Previous Seasons Played Flag Football: 1
- Other Sports Played: Track and Field
- Three Words That Describe Madi: Explosive, Instinctive, Comical

I decided to play flag football in high school because I enjoyed playing in junior high school. I had also competed in cross country in junior high, but flag football was a more enjoyable experience for me. I like how flag football relies on a multitude of skill sets when compared to running sports. You must be agile and reactive and have eye-hand coordination, all while going at top speed, reaching out to grab a flag or catch a ball. I also liked how it kept me in shape for the track and field season.

I loved the camaraderie of GFF and how close the team was to each other. There is a spot for everyone that matches their abilities. Playing a new sport helps with learning life skills that can be used on and off the field. Sometimes, it was challenging. I had to learn a new position as a wide receiver in addition to playing safety. That just helped me develop my self-confidence.

Flag football is a milestone for women's sports. Although similar to other sports, participating in flag football allows us to develop skills we didn't have before. I think having flag football as a sport for girls is important. It represents an ongoing change in women's sports. Being a part of a sport that is changing societal norms has improved my self-worth. My overall takeaway is that my freshman year of flag football was one of the best experiences of my life. I will never forget all the amazing teammates I got to play with and what I was a part of for women in sports.

Coach Denise

I first met Madi as a 7th grader when she ran cross country. She came out with one friend, and they were usually quiet and stuck together. I wasn't sure when I first joked if she knew I was teasing. Ends up that her sense of humor is fantastic. She'd laugh at my silly jokes and was deadpan when I was sarcastic. And sometimes, when I am trying to explain something, it doesn't come out quite right. You know that look someone gives you when they think you are a little crazy? She has mastered that, and I have been a frequent recipient. As she once said, "Aren't we all <a little crazy>?"

I love that Madi talked about how her self-confidence has grown through sports. In 7th grade, she was one of our fastest cross-country runners but tended to spend time with just her one friend, worried about not being fast enough. So, when she came out for flag football, I thought, "She's going to be timid." But as she spent time in the position of safety, I watched her skill and confidence develop. By the time she came to high school, she was immersed in a group of friends and began to play more confidently. I look forward to watching this grow over the next few years.

Be brave. Do hard things. Believe.

Although Madi didn't specially answer this question, we have seen her be brave. She is a defensive player, who plays in the secondary, sitting back to watch the play develop. She's comfortable there. She'd prefer not to play offense. But we required her to take reps as a wide receiver. She described that even though this was hard for her, it helped her develop confidence. We look forward to seeing her progress as she continues to believe in herself on this side of the ball.

Mia: Captain

- Position: Rusher, Center
- All League: Honorable Mention
- Team Award: #makingherstory
- Class: Junior
- Previous Seasons Played Flag Football: 0
- Other Sports Played: Cross Country, Track
- Three Words That Describe Mia: Charismatic, Entertaining, Empathetic

I chose to play flag football because I needed an outlet. Although I had been running cross country and participating in track, I had been sidelined from team sports with chronic pain. I had some personal challenges to overcome, but I felt comfortable playing flag football. I was looking forward to experiencing a team sport again. The team dynamic on the field differed from what I had previously experienced. "It was a second chance that was a fresh start; it was a new beginning, and it was what I needed in my life."

Having flag football available to female high school athletes broke the barrier to a sport they hadn't previously had. We were often on the sideline watching our male peers, my boyfriend included, playing tackle football. The introduction of flag football as a CIF sport provides a whole new world for females, usually reserved for males. This option can change the future for some of these athletes. It promotes equity, equality, and empowerment. Every game taught me something about myself and the person I want to be. It reminds us that girls can do anything boys can do.

Coach Denise

Long after the end of many of our summer practices, Mia would be on the field, having long conversations with the coaches. These were not the usual "Coach, how can I do better at pulling a flag?" talks, but deep and inspired talks about her ideas for team bonding, being a better person, equity, and humanity. I credit Mia with the idea for me to share an "empowherment" quote with the team in our pre-game huddles. When discussing building the momentum of #makingherstory, Mia said, "You should start each game with a quote." She exemplified to her teammates how we want our players to behave on and off the field. Unsurprisingly, her peers elected her to be a team captain.

Mia took advantage of this opportunity to be back on the field playing a team sport. Before practices started, she'd have fun with new friends, listen to music, and laugh about the day's events. It was a while before I knew the internal growth she was experiencing. In our first game, the intensity of play was at a level different than scrimmages between teammates. It took many of our players by surprise. Knowing that Mia managed her pain while playing, I gave her extra time to process the intensity, and then, after discussing it with her, moved her from center (offense) to rush (defense). When we played this opponent later in the season, I was careful to monitor Mia's interaction, worried she'd feel intimidated after our first contest. I gave her the option of staying on defense. But she asked to play on offense and went on the field with a brave heart and tenacity that showed tremendous growth. We give an award acknowledging an athlete who brings qualities to the team that we want players to emulate as humans on and off the field, including "being someone brave, who does hard things, and who believes." For these qualities, Mia earned the #makingherstory award.

Be brave. Do hard things. Believe.

Mia's bravery included addressing physical pain. Participating in GFF showed her that she can deal with chronic pain, even on days when it feels impossible. She learned she had an inner strength that she didn't know existed and that she can do things she never thought possible. Mia was brave many times this season as she learned how to balance her physical well-being with participating with the team. According to Mia, playing GFF, "Has taught me to enjoy every moment and be truly present in the now. I was extra grateful this season to be able to happily and healthily move my body." This lesson, plus spending time with her teammates and coaches, gave her joy."

Mikayla

- Position: QB and Corner
- Class: Freshman
- Previous Seasons Played Flag Football: 0
- Other Sports Played: Softball, Basketball, Soccer, Tae Kwon Do
- Three Words That Describe Mikayla: Motivated, Cheerful, Energetic

My favorite part of flag football was working through how I saw my skills when compared to others, with the support of my teammates/friends. I remember I would watch our other quarterbacks, Gaby and Dakota, and think how amazing they are! How will I be that good? And I doubted it would happen. Throughout the season, I worked on my throwing skills and trying to determine if my pass was "cloudy or clear." (That's how we refer to looking for the open receiver.) My teammates supported me and helped me see that I could achieve something big with hard work and determination.

I play many sports, but I remember the boys always telling me that I couldn't play football because I was a girl. When I decided to play GFF, I was told it wouldn't be as interesting to watch because, unlike tackle football, it didn't have much contact. (It is a noncontact sport.) But those people were wrong. It is an interesting and fun sport to watch and play, growing across the country. The thought of playing tackle against people twice my size wasn't reasonable. But flag football is a way to encourage more girls to try this team-focused sport.

The community we created in our team was different from my other sports. We all supported each other while learning and growing together. It was a safe environment where we all spoke positively to one another. GFF is a great sport where you build strong relationships and bonds with your teammates. It gives girls the opportunity to play a form of football. And, for those people who said I couldn't do it, it was amazing to prove them wrong.

Coach Denise

Mikayla may be the busiest of our athletes. She constantly runs from one sporting practice to another or leaves a GFF game to play in a soccer tournament. Not only is she a multisport athlete, but she also has a Tae Kwon Do practice and keeps herself ready for Junior Guards (the summer lifeguard camp) by swimming and surfing. I don't know how she does it. On top of all her busyness, she works hard to learn her new skills.

Using her skill, Mikayla has the physical ability to throw the long ball and continues to improve on finding the open receiver. She has the insight to let us know if her pass was cloudy or clear. But the thing is, she has value on both sides of the ball and in many positions. She is a great example of why college coaches report preferring multisport athletes. She is quick, agile, and can play multiple positions on our team. And, no matter where we ask her to play, she is just happy to be out playing football.

Be brave. Do hard things. Believe.

Mikayla's response to this is succinct. She reminds us that people may make any one of us doubt that we can do something. But she reminds us that we have to learn not to listen to the disbelievers and those who don't positively support us. The best response is to believe you can do it and prove them wrong.

Nancy

- Positions: Center, Safety
- All League: 2nd Team
- Team Award: Offensive Player
- Class: Season
- Previous Seasons Played Flag Football: 3
- Other Sports Played: Volleyball, Wrestling, Track
- Three Words About Nancy: Physical, Sensitive, Adaptable

I decided to play flag football because I was looking for a new experience, a new team without a long history together. In my previous sports, there wasn't a lot of team bonding, but we did a lot with GFF. I really enjoyed that. It fostered building relationships with each other, and that led to trust. Because I trusted my teammates, we were more in sync and performed better.

I loved that our team included all grade levels. The underclassmen looked up to us as leaders, and I was so proud of them and their successes. We always enjoyed listening to music and singing while hanging out before practice. At team bonding, we made s'mores and talked to people we wouldn't have met otherwise. I bawled on Senior Night because I had made friends with these younger players and would miss playing with them.

Playing flag football taught me a lot about tackle football. My brother played football in high school, but I didn't understand the game. When I watch it now, I know what is happening on the field. I would have never played tackle football for fear of getting hurt but also because, as a girl, I probably wouldn't get playing time. Although flag football isn't exactly the same as tackle, since it is non-contact, it provides an opportunity for girls to play football. It's one thing to talk about equity in sports, but this opportunity to play this sport is an example of actions speaking louder than words.

Coach Denise

When you first meet Nancy, she is quiet, almost tentative, but she greets you with the kindest smile. It is this sweetness that resonates with me when I think of Nancy. Right before the start of the school year, we had an end-of-summer team bonding. The upperclassmen told the freshmen about the campus on a hill. They were giving them tips on how to get to classes on time and where different locations were. The next day, at freshman orientation, some of the older players met the younger players to help them find their classes. It was a heartwarming example of humans supporting one another through kind and generous actions.

In contrast, when you put flags on her and a football in her hands, she becomes a different person. Nancy was one of two players we would remind that pulling a flag or gaining a few extra yards wasn't worth sacrificing their body. She is a strong and intentional competitor who wants to do her best for her team. She became our go-to player when we needed just a few yards. More often than not, she turned that few yards into many, one of the leaders in yards gained. Our AD even renamed one of our plays to "The Nancy," because she was so successful at it. For this and her team commitment, she won the Offensive Player award.

Be brave. Do hard things. Believe.

Nancy described her reservations about coming out to play this new sport were that she wouldn't be good enough. This came from having played in another sport where she was replaced by another player. But she bravely came out and worked hard to learn the rules and the routes. In one of our last games, we moved her to play defense as a safety in a game where the score was close. She felt the pressure to make sure the opponent didn't score. When the ball was passed to a player that was taller than her, she jumped and deflected the ball, preventing that player from scoring. When discussing this play, Nancy said, "I don't always see in myself when I have done something good. But, this time, I knew I had done something right, and I liked how that felt."

Natasha

- Position: Wide Receiver, Center
- Class of 2025
- Previous Seasons Played Flag Football: 0
- Other Sports Played: Soccer, Tae Kwon Do, Track
- Three Words About Natasha: Stealthy, Motivated, Reliable

I decided to play flag football because it had just been sanctioned as a high school sport, and it was exciting to be part of an inaugural team! I had never played before and was eager to learn a new sport and meet new people! I was also inspired to play alongside my friends and make lasting memories of my experiences at AHS! I am honored to have taken part in this first CIF season for GFF! As a new sport brought to high schools throughout California, I was thrilled to represent AHS. It was a wonderful experience and an incredible opportunity for women. Although football is considered a more masculine sport, the option to participate in GFF is really empowering for women and opens the door for greater sports equality and inclusion! I look forward to it becoming more available at high schools and colleges across the country.

The hardest part about playing GFF was that it was a new sport for me. It took some time to accustom myself to it since it differed from the sports I had played. I was unfamiliar with the rules of the game and how to run a play or work defense. Compared to soccer, the field was smaller, physical contact was not allowed, and I had to adjust to the stop-and-go pace of running plays. But I also found many skills like footwork, quick decision-making, change of speed, acceleration, and fake-outs crossed over to flag football, which soon "clicked" for me. Another difference—but a very positive one—is that the playing environment is much more fun, positive, and less stressful. The community of players is also much more closely knit!

Many things were special about playing GFF. The team, the opportunity for girls, the learning of a new sport. Some specific games, however, stood out more than others. Historically, "Homecoming" games are for the tackle football team with large crowds at Friday Night Lights. Our school's athletics and activities director expanded homecoming to include GFF. It was an exciting game that ended 6-0 with a pass to me for the game-winning touchdown! But equally memorable was our homecoming crowd, which had many people attending and cheering us on at this game. I loved the show of support we received from our AHS community.

Coach Denise

Natasha's contribution to our team was multifold. The first quality that comes to mind when thinking of Natasha is how engaging she is. Her kind and humorous spirit makes it easy to have a conversation with her. And she genuinely laughs when we make jokes, or I do my "two-flags" jig. But that shouldn't deter anyone from recognizing her fierce and reliable contribution to our team. I am pretty sure that out on the field, she effectively "tackles" (flag pulls) the offensive player and then gives them a friendly smile as she hands the flag back to them. Ask her to sub into a position that isn't her usual, or get the balls into her hand, and you know you have set your team up for success.

The bond developed with this team was remarkable and moving. Many of the players mentioned it in these interviews. As Natasha noted, being a part of this team was an opportunity to "make last memories." Perhaps it was the novelty of the sport, with the learning curve high for everyone. It could also be team-bonding activities that began in the summer and continued throughout the season. Without regional and state playoffs, the pressure to win wasn't as great. It was definitely a reflection of our team goal of empowering the humans who committed to playing. It also reflected players like Natasha, who created a friendly and inclusive team environment.

Be brave. Do hard things. Believe.

Natasha reminds us that in life, it is important to venture out, try new things, and challenge yourself! If she hadn't been brave enough to try this sport, she says she wouldn't have known how much fun playing is and would have missed the chance to be a part of this team. Taking this chance helped her develop confidence and believe in herself. By bravely trying new things, the sky's the limit for what a person wants to achieve.

Nina: Captain

- Position: Middle Back, Center
- Class: Senior
- Seasons Played Flag Football: 1
- Other Sports Played: Track
- Three Words That Describe Nina: Coachable, Motivated, Instructive

Girls Flag Football at Aptos High School was my first year ever playing a team sport. The first day of summer practice was one of the hardest, as it was hard for me to open up and be social. I almost didn't show up because I thought I wouldn't know anyone, and people would think I was weird. (Coach Denise's interjection, "I think this was very brave.")

Playing flag football was a challenge at first, especially compared to "easier" sports like track. It demanded more challenging training and a higher level of focus, pushing me out of my comfort zone while I learned coverage and routes. To be safe and successful, we had to know each other's moves on the field, and this improved as we developed camaraderie. I loved how we supported each other and brought each other up as friends and fellow women at practices and on the sidelines at games, where we were always loud and cheered. In addition to building these friendships, playing flag football improved my track performance. In the spring, I felt more confident, strong, and agile in track after my season on the flag football team.

One of my favorite memories from the season was the homecoming week game. Homecoming was special because it was the first time our flag football team was honored and celebrated by our school community. The whole school came together for the annual homecoming parade around the track during the halftime of our "Thursday night lights" game. We felt so special, and having a huge crowd watching us play was exhilarating.

Coach Denise

Nina showed up for summer practices and was highly motivated to learn a new sport. On the field, she was focused as she implemented the coaches' instructions. She took great care in learning new skills and plays through the repetition offered at practice. When a teammate was unsure which route to run or how to provide defensive coverage, Nina would guide them. Off the field, she took on a leadership role of helping organize activities and fundraisers. In our first year, players voted for captains, and for her dedication, Nina's teammates voted for her as one of our captains.

The following is an excerpt from Nina's college applications describing the impact of flag football: "With pink ribbons in our hair, we walked onto the field each day with a sense of purpose. We may have looked like a simple high school team, but for us there was a deeper meaning. It felt as if we were representing millions of women who lived before us; those prevented from living their lives due to oppressive and patriarchal worldly systems. I truly believe that my flag football experience changed my perspective on what empowered girls can achieve. It taught me to never let societal norms dampen my curiosity and to always push myself to try new things, regardless of what others may think or say."

Be brave. Do hard things. Believe.

Nina encourages us never to be afraid to chase something that interests us. She says to be brave, and don't fear what people think of you. It was hard for her to walk on the field that first day of summer practice, doing something new with people she didn't know. According to her, "When you overcome that barrier (something I am still working on), the world opens up infinite possibilities."

Siena

- Position: Safety, Wide Receiver
- All League: Honorable Mention
- Team Award: Defensive Player
- Class: Junior
- Previous Seasons Played Flag Football: ½ (interrupted by COVID-19 Shelter in Place)
- Other Sports Played: Track and Field
- Three Words That Describe Siena: Tough, Gritty, Strong

I have always loved football. It has been a big part of my entire life. My dad is a Steelers fan, and we have that in common. I love the game so much. Running around, following the ball, anticipating the plays—I love it all. I loved playing it in junior high, but sadly, that season was cut short due to COVID-19. I knew Coach Denise from the junior high team and loved her, so I knew I would have an amazing coach. My favorite part of the whole experience was playing football.

Some of my favorite memories from the season are when everyone cheered us on. The games we lost were always competitive. Our coaches used those losses to identify what we needed to practice so that we could get better. I know that winning isn't everything but winning all our league games felt amazing.

Flag football is more team-oriented than other sports I have played. You work together and communicate constantly if you are going to have success. And it's amazing to have flag football available to girls. Tackle football has been so celebrated in our society, and girls deserve a chance to play the game and receive the same praise. Having Girls' Flag Football as a varsity high school sport creates more opportunities for girls to be involved in sports and provides another step towards respect for women's sports.

Coach Denise

I remember meeting Siena at the junior high for our cut-short flag football season. She was this tiny, cheerful player with a defensive attitude incongruent with her disposition and size. I was excited to coach her in the position of safety, but then our season was taken away by the 2020 shutdown. Having the chance to coach her again when she came out for flag football at the high school thrilled me. I watched as she made "new connections and became closer with old friends and created new ones" and could see her happiness. The social isolation that came with the pandemic was depressing and isolating for many students, and sports were a welcome outlet for connection. Her mom commented on the positive post-pandemic changes the season had made for Siena. I was so excited that Siena had the chance to be back on the gridiron playing flag football.

Siena deserves recognition for her contribution to the season record. She led the team in deflections and was second in interceptions, which was remarkable since opponents often stopped sending passes to her side of the field. In one close game, as many of them were, there were seconds left on the clock, and the opponents just needed one big play to win. That wasn't going to happen on Siena's watch, and when the deep pass came her way, she intercepted it in the end zone. Then, she enjoyed the cheering that erupted as we won the game. She did all of this with a sprained hand, and it was for this and her positive contribution to the team that she was awarded Defensive Player.

Be brave. Do hard things. Believe.

Siena highlights how the fear of failure is a barrier for people to try new things. She says, "I have always been fearful of failure." Reflecting on this quote helped her to recognize this fear in herself. But she came out for GFF, and it helped her overcome this fear. She told me, "I loved this entire experience; the game; the team; the coach."

Valerie

- Position: Running Back, Corner
- Class: Freshman
- Previous Seasons Played Flag Football: 1
- Other Sports Played: None
- Three Words That Describe Val: Fast, Durable, Tenacious

Having the opportunity to play flag football means a lot to me. I decided to play in high school because my junior high flag football experience went so well. I wanted to continue playing the sport because it's a really fun game. We get to run around, being chased when we have a ball and chasing opponents to pull their flags. Every time I play, I am happy and excited. I also wanted to make friends as a freshman in high school. I did, and they are amazing! I did this on the FIRST EVER AHS flag football team as part of the expansion of flag football in California.

As exciting as flag football is to play, what I enjoyed the most was bonding with my teams. Whether at practices or playing games, we always had a fun time. It is just fun to stay active and build teamwork skills while playing flag football. My favorite memories of the season involved being with the team. One of these memories is of my teammates and I working together to organize a bake sale. We made and sold all the food ourselves, fundraising for uniforms and equipment while enjoying being together.

Now that GFF is a high school sport, girls who have been interested in playing football have an opportunity to participate in a sport that has mostly been exclusively played by boys. This is a safer alternative to tackle football for girls while still offering the excitement, thrill, and skills of the game. I am so happy that more girls have the opportunity to play this fun sport. Playing is not just about the game itself, but about friendships, teamwork, and opportunities for girls.

Coach Denise

When I think of Val, I start singing the 1970s jingle, "Weebles Wobble, and they don't fall down." Picture this. Val, who in size, is one of our smaller players, is out on the field on the day of our first league competition in her position of corner. An offensive player comes running full speed towards Val. Val sets her feet, prepared to pull at least one flag. In many contests, we are playing against athletes who haven't played flag football before. As they learn a new sport, there is a period when they are still working on skills like deceleration and agile cuts. The offensive player inadvertently runs right through Val, who literally goes down to the ground and between the ball-holding player's legs. There was a collective gasp and shouts from the sidelines, "Are you ok?" But, up hops Val, hand above her head, proudly holding a flag.

Reading through these interviews, two things have become apparent. One is that, at least on this team, the players really enjoyed being a part of a team of peers sharing this lived experience. The other is that, although by rules, girls are allowed to play tackle football, many do not play in high school due to the physical nature and the general size difference between boys and girls by that age. But just because they haven't played football doesn't mean they haven't wanted to. These players recognize the gender disparity that has existed. They recognized in this inaugural year of GFF in California that they truly were "#makingherstory."

Be Brave. Do Hard Things. Believe.

Growing as an athlete and a person requires not letting making mistakes be a barrier. Val told me that when she doesn't play well or makes a mistake, she overthinks what she has done and loses confidence. It's hard to keep playing when upset about an error. Playing GFF has taught Val that these mistakes can be used to help a person train harder and that is how you can improve.

Fourth Quarter: The Final Whistle

How Did It End?

Our season ended with hugs and tears and laughter and love. The final score didn't matter (much) because the real win was in the program we had started together. We knew when we gathered one last time on the A in the middle of our football field, that it was the end of this experience we had created together. Nothing could take away from us what our hard work that started in the warm evenings of the summer allowed us to accomplish during the crisp days of fall. Each team member bravely came to our program to be a part of this new experience of high school girls flag football.

More importantly than our individual and team achievements, we were a part of a group of teams in our league, across California, and in other states across the nation who are looking for ways to promote equity. Gender equity continues to lag for women. But, slowly more opportunities are becoming available. Offering a new sport to girls and women, particularly one that is similar to a version dominated by boys and men, creates another option for them to participate. Girls flag football is growing exponentially across the nation, moving us one step closer to the vision set forth by Title IX.

Going into that last game, as the captains returned from the coin toss, we got into our final pre-game huddle. Before each game, we started with a quote, before the captains broke us with an "Aptos on me, Aptos on three" cheer. That day, the quote was my own, as I looked at my players who were one game away from being undefeated in league and said, "be brave, do hard things, believe."

The scoreboard showed our hard-fought win with a final score of 7-0 that last game, an exciting end to what was an incredible and memorable season. These athletes had been brave, they had done a hard thing, and their success came because they believed.

Pre-Game Quotes

- "Who run the world? Girls" - Beyonce
- *"There is no force more powerful than a woman determined to rise." – Dorothy Dandridge*
- "The question isn't who's going to let me; it's who is going to stop me." - Ayn Rand
- *"A girl should be two things: who and what she wants." - Coco Chanel*
- "I raise up my voice-not so that I can shout, but so that those without a voice can be heard...we cannot succeed when half of us are held back." - Malala Yousafzai

- *"Women are always saying, 'We can do anything that men can do.' But men should be saying, 'We can do anything that women can do.'" - Gloria Steinem*

- "It is impossible to live without failing at something, unless you live so cautiously that you might as well not have lived at all-in which case, you fail by default."- JK Rowling
- *"I have no difficulty holding logic and feeling at the same time. And it does not diminish my powers; it expands them." - Lawyer Barbie*

- "I don't really think about the degree of difficulty or the possibility of making a mistake. I just try to relax and let my preparation and training take over." - Simone BIles

- *"You never know if you can actually do something against all odds until you actually do it." - Abby Wambach*

- "The only person who can stop you from reaching your goals is you." - Jackie Joyner Kersee

- *"I have learned that as long as I hold fast to my beliefs and values - and follow my own moral compass - then the only expectations I need to live up to are my own." - Michelle Obama*

- "It is our choices that show what we truly are, far more than our abilities." – Dumbledore
- *"Don't wait until you've reached your goal to be proud of yourself. Be proud of every step you take toward reaching that goal." - Simone Biles*

- "Be brave. Do hard things. Believe." - Coach Denise

Play Along Answer Key

The one most likely not to get called for flag guarding	Ava (Gavin)
The one most likely to be a future coach	Nina
The one most likely to catch every QBs pass	Angelique
The one most likely to forget her water bottle	Ellie
The one most likely to lower her shoulder	Nancy
The one most likely to make Denise do a jig	Elenah
The one most likely to play flag football in Europe	Emi
The one most likely to tackle the QB	Mia P
The one most likely to throw the long ball	Mikayla
The one most likely to give her teammates or coach a hug	Siena
The one who always bring positivity to the field	Ashlyn
The one who embodies a goldfish	Gaby
The one who embodies being a football player	Dakota
The one who found her spot at safety	June
The one who gets along with everyone	Janelle
The one who gets knocked over and pops right back up	Val
The one who lights up the team with happy	Maddie B
The one who perseveres	Alexa
The one who quietly creates offensive success	Natasha
The one who reminds us that football is fun	Annika
The one whose actions speak louder than words	Lauren
The one whose face never lies	Madi P
The one whose hips DO lie	Izzy
The one you can depend on	Julia

Overtime (References)

◇ Gatorade Sports Science Institute (nd). *The unevenness of social change in women's sports in the United States: Historical and contemporary perspectives.*

◇ Graham, P. (2024, January 3). *Flag football will debut at 2028 LA games and may feature NFL starts. Here's what to know about the sport.* NBCLA.

◇ Hong, C. (2023, March 22). *Girls flag football newly sanctioned as state sport for the fall.* The Campanile.

◇ International Women's Flag Football Association (nd). *Who we are.*

◇ Niehoff, K. (2024, April 10). *Flag Football Expanding Nationwide as Next Emerging High School Sports for Girls.* National Federation of State High School Associations (NFHS).

◇ Ohanian, P. (2023, June 2). *Why college coaches prefer multi-sport athletes.* Sports Engine.

◇ Van Cleave, K., & Novak, A. (2024, January 26). *Flag football is skyrocketing in popularity nationwide-And it's not just for boys.* CBS News.

◇ White, G. (nd). *Which colleges have women's flag football teams? And how to get involved.* GMTM.

◇ Yu, C. (2023). *Up to speed: The groundbreaking science of women athletes.* Riverhead Books.

About the Author

Dr. Denise Calafato Russo is a college nutrition professor at a Hispanic-serving institution. She has spent the past two decades transforming her classrooms using equitable teaching practices to support a diverse population of students. She takes this same passion for equity to the flag football field, where she supports the opportunity for girls to play football. In her downtime, Denise enjoys doing sports-related activities with her husband and three grown children, all of whom have been involved in a wide variety of sports, including flag football.